T0383055

Acquiring Online Management Reports

Acquiring Online Management Reports has been co-published simultaneously as *The Acquisitions Librarian,* Number 24 2000.

The Acquisitions Librarian Monographic "Separates"

Below is a list of "separates," which in serials librarianship means a special issue simultaneously published as a special journal issue or double-issue *and* as a "separate" hardbound monograph. (This is a format which we also call a "DocuSerial.")

"Separates" are published because specialized libraries or professionals may wish to purchase a specific thematic issue by itself in a format which can be separately cataloged and shelved, as opposed to purchasing the journal on an on-going basis. Faculty members may also more easily consider a "separate" for classroom adoption.

"Separates" are carefully classified separately with the major book jobbers so that the journal tie-in can be noted on new book order slips to avoid duplicate purchasing.

You may wish to visit Haworth's website at . . .

http://www.haworthpressinc.com

. . . to search our online catalog for complete tables of contents of these separates and related publications.

You may also call 1-800-HAWORTH (outside US/Canada: 607-722-5857), or Fax: 1-800-895-0582 (outside US/Canada: 607-771-0012), or e-mail at:

getinfo@haworthpressinc.com

Acquiring Online Management Reports, edited by William E. Jarvis (No. 24, 2000). *This fact-filled guide explores a broad variety of issues involving acquisitions and online management reports to keep librarians and library managers current with changing technology and, ultimately, offer patrons more information. This book provides you with discussions and suggestions on several topics, including working with vendors, developing cost-effective collection development methods to suit your library, assessing collection growth, and choosing the best electronic resources to help meet your goals. Acquiring Online Management Reports offers you an array of proven ideas, options, and examples that will enable your library to keep up with client demands and simplify the process of collecting, maintaining, and interpreting online reports.*

The Internet and Acquisitions: Sources and Resources for Development, edited by Mary E. Timmons (No. 23, 2000). *"For those trying to determine how the Internet could be of use to their particular library in the area of acquisitions, or for those who have already decided they should be moving in that direction . . . this volume is a good place to begin." (James Mitchell, MLS, Library Director, Bainbridge-Guilford Central School, Bainbridge, NY)*

Gifts and Exchanges: Problems, Frustrations, . . . and Triumphs, edited by Catherine Denning (No. 22, 1999). *"A complete compendium embracing all aspects of the matter in articles that are uniformly well-written by people experienced in this field." (Jonathan S. Tryon, CAL, JD, Professor, Graduate School of Library and Information Studies, University of Rhode Island)*

Periodical Acquisitions and the Internet, edited by Nancy Slight-Gibney (No. 21, 1999). *Sheds light on the emerging trends in selection, acquisition, and access to electronic journals.*

Public Library Collection Development in the Information Age, edited by Annabel K. Stephens (No. 20, 1998). *"A first-rate collection of articles . . . This is an engaging and helpful work for anyone involved in developing public library collections." (Lyn Hopper, MLn, Director, Chestatee Regional Library, Dahlonega, Georgia)*

Fiction Acquisition/Fiction Management: Education and Training, edited by Georgine N. Olson (No. 19, 1998). *"It is about time that attention is given to the collection in public libraries. . . it is about time that public librarians be encouraged to treat recreational reading with the same respect that is paid to informational reading . . .Thank you to Georgine Olson for putting this volume together." (Regan Robinson, MLS, Editor and Publisher, Librarian Collection Letter)*

Acquisitions and Collection Development in the Humanities, edited by Irene Owens (No. 17/18, 1997). *"CAN EASILY BECOME A PERSONAL REFERENCE TOOL."* (*William D. Cunningham, PhD, Retired faculty, College of Library and Information Service, University of Maryland, College Park*)

Approval Plans: Issues and Innovations, edited by John H. Sandy (No. 16, 1996). *"This book is valuable for several reasons, the primary one being that librarians in one-person libraries need to know how approval plans work before they can try one for their particular library. . . An important addition to the professional literature."* (*The One-Person Library*)

Current Legal Issues in Publishing, edited by A. Bruce Strauch (No. 15, 1996). *"Provides valuable access to a great deal of information about the current state of copyright thinking."* (*Library Association Record*)

New Automation Technology for Acquisitions and Collection Development, edited by Rosann Bazirjian (No. 13/14, 1995). *"Rosann Bazirjian has gathered together 13 current practitioners who explore technology and automation in acquisitions and collection development. . . CONTAINS SOMETHING FOR EVERYONE."* (*Library Acquisitions: Practice and Theory*)

Management and Organization of the Acquisitions Department, edited by Twyla Racz and Rosina Tammany (No. 12, 1994). *"Brings together topics and librarians from across the country to discuss some basic challenges and changes facing our profession today."* (*Library Acquisitions: Practice and Theory*)

A. V. in Public and School Libraries: Selection and Policy Issues, edited by Margaret J. Hughes and Bill Katz (No. 11, 1994). *"Many points of view are brought forward for those who are creating new policy or procedural documents. . . Provide[s] firsthand experience as well as considerable background knowledge . . . ."* (*Australian Library Review*)

Multicultural Acquisitions, edited by Karen Parrish and Bill Katz (No. 9/10, 1993). *"A stimulating overview of the U.S. multicultural librarianship scene."* (*The Library Assn. Reviews*)

Popular Culture and Acquisitions, edited by Allen Ellis (No. 8, 1993). *"A provocative penetrating set of chapters on the tricky topic of popular culture acquisitions. . . A valuable guidebook."* (*Journal of Popular Culture*)

Collection Assessment: A Look at the RLG Conspectus©, edited by Richard J. Wood and Katina Strauch (No. 7, 1992). *"A well-organized, thorough book . . . Provides the most realistic representations of what the Conspectus is and what its limitations are . . . Will take an important place in Conspectus literature."* (*Library Acquisitions: Practice & Theory*)

Evaluating Acquisitions and Collections Management, edited by Pamela S. Cenzer and Cynthia I. Gozzi (No. 6, 1991). *"With the current emphasis on evaluation and return on funding, the material is timely indeed!"* (*Library Acquisitions: Practice & Theory*)

Vendors and Library Acquisitions, edited by Bill Katz (No. 5, 1991). *"Should be required reading for all new acquisitions librarians and all library science students who plan a career in technical services. As a whole it is a very valuable resource."* (*Library Acquisitions: Practice & Theory*)

Operational Costs in Acquisitions, edited by James R. Coffey (No. 4, 1991). *"For anyone interested in embarking on a cost study of the acquisitions process this book will be worthwhile reading."* (*Library Acquisitions: Practice & Theory*)

Legal and Ethical Issues in Acquisitions, edited by Katina Strauch and A. Bruce Strauch (No. 3, 1990). *"This excellent compilation is recommended to both collection development/acquisition librarians and library administrators in academic libraries."* (*The Journal of Academic Librarianship*)

The Acquisitions Budget, edited by Bill Katz (No. 2, 1989). *"Practical advice and tips are offered throughout . . . Those new to acquisitions work, especially in academic libraries, will find the book useful background reading."* (*Library Association Record*)

Automated Acquisitions: Issues for the Present and Future, edited by Amy Dykeman (No. 1, 1989). *"This book should help librarians to learn from the experience of colleagues in choosing the system that best suits their local requirements. . . [It] will appeal to library managers as well as to library school faculty and students."* (*Library Association Record*)

Published by

The Haworth Information Press, 10 Alice Street, Binghamton, NY 13904-1580

The Haworth Information Press is an imprint of The Haworth Press, Inc., 10 Alice Street, Binghamton, NY 13904-1580 USA.

Acquiring Online Management Reports has been co-published simultaneously as *The Acquisitions Librarian*™, Number 24 2000.

The development, preparation, and publication of this work has been undertaken with great care. However, the publisher, employees, editors, and agents of The Haworth Press and all imprints of The Haworth Press, Inc., including The Haworth Medical Press® and Pharmaceutical Products Press®, are not responsible for any errors contained herein or for consequences that may ensue from use of materials or information contained in this work. Opinions expressed by the author(s) are not necessarily those of The Haworth Press, Inc.

Cover design by Thomas J. Mayshock Jr.

Library of Congress Cataloging-in-Publication Data

Acquiring online management reports / William E. Jarvis, editor.
　　　p. cm.
　　　"Has been co-published simultaneously as The acquisitions librarian, no. 24, 2000."
　　　Includes bibliographical references and index.
　　　ISBN 0-7890-0698-7 (acid-free paper)
　　　1. Acquisition of serial publications–United States–Electronic information resources. 2. Acquisition of electronic journals–United States. 3. Research libraries–Acquisitions–United States–Electronic information resources. 4. Collection management (Libraries)–United States–Electronic information resources. 5. Library statistics–United States–Electronic information resources. I. Jarvis, William E., 1945- II. Acquisitions librarian.

Z692.S5 A29 2000
025.2′832–dc21   00-031934

Acquiring Online Management Reports

William E. Jarvis
Editor

Acquiring Online Management Reports has been co-published simultaneously as *The Acquisitions Librarian*, Number 24 2000.

The Haworth Information Press
An Imprint of
The Haworth Press, Inc.
New York • London • Oxford

INDEXING & ABSTRACTING

Contributions to this publication are selectively indexed or abstracted in print, electronic, online, or CD-ROM version(s) of the reference tools and information services listed below. This list is current as of the copyright date of this publication. See the end of this section for additional notes.

- *BUBL Information Service, an Internet-based Information Service for the UK higher education community <URL: http://bubl.ac.uk/>*
- *Central Library & Documentation Bureau*
- *CNPIEC Reference Guide: Chinese National Directory of Foreign Periodicals*
- *Combined Health Information Database (CHID)*
- *Current Awareness Abstracts of Library & Information Management Literature, ASLIB (UK)*
- *Educational Administration Abstracts (EAA)*
- *FINDEX, free Internet Directory of over 150,000 publications from around the world www.publist.com*
- *Herbal Connection, The "Abstracts Section" http://www.herbnet.com*
- *IBZ International Bibliography of Periodical Literature*
- *Index to Periodical Articles Related to Law*
- *Information Reports & Bibliographies*
- *Information Science Abstracts*
- *Informed Librarian, The <http://www.infosourcespub.com>*
- *INSPEC*
- *Journal of Academic Librarianship: Guide to Professional Literature, The*
- *Konyvtari Figyelo-Library Review*
- *Library & Information Science Abstracts (LISA)*
- *Library and Information Science Annual (LISCA) www.lu.com/arba*
- *Library Literature*

(continued)

- *Microcomputer Abstracts can be found Online at: DIALOG, File 233; HRIN & OCLC and on Internet at: Cambridge Scientific Abstracts; Dialog Web; & OCLC.*

- *National Clearinghouse on Child Abuse & Neglect Information http://www.calib.com/nccanch*

- *Newsletter of Library and Information Services*

- *NIAAA Alcohol and Alcohol Problems Science Database (ETOH)*

- *PASCAL, c/o Institute de L'Information Scientifique et Technique http://www.inist.fr*

- *REHABDATA, National Rehabilitation Information Center (NARIC) http://www.naric.com/naric*

- *Social Services Abstracts http://www.csa.com*

- *Sociological Abstracts http://www.csa.com*

Special Bibliographic Notes related to special journal issues (separates) and indexing/abstracting:

- indexing/abstracting services in this list will also cover material in any "separate" that is co-published simultaneously with Haworth's special thematic journal issue or DocuSerial. Indexing/abstracting usually covers material at the article/chapter level.

- monographic co-editions are intended for either non-subscribers or libraries which intend to purchase a second copy for their circulating collections.

- monographic co-editions are reported to all jobbers/wholesalers/approval plans. The source journal is listed as the "series" to assist the prevention of duplicate purchasing in the same manner utilized for books-in-series.

- to facilitate user/access services all indexing/abstracting services are encouraged to utilize the co-indexing entry note indicated at the bottom of the first page of each article/chapter/contribution.

- this is intended to assist a library user of any reference tool (whether print, electronic, online, or CD-ROM) to locate the monographic version if the library has purchased this version but not a subscription to the source journal.

- individual articles/chapters in any Haworth publication are also available through the Haworth Document Delivery Service (HDDS).

Acquiring Online Management Reports

CONTENTS

ABOUT THE EDITOR

William E. Jarvis is a faculty librarian (associate professor level) at Washington State University, Pullman, WA, where he served as Acquisitions Librarian from 1990 to 1999, and is now Collection Services Librarian there. He has been in library service for over 20 years, including over 15 years in collection management and acquisitions work. Mr. Jarvis has long been involved in a wide variety of ALA activities, including ALCTS work. He researches and publishes on a wide variety of information studies topics ranging from online library processing operations to interdisciplinary time capsule studies.

Acquiring Online Management Reports: An Editorial Introduction

William E. Jarvis

The scope of this volume is a very broad one, and, indeed, is as open-ended as the changing, developing set of roles that encompass acquisitions librarianship and the vagaries of collection management. It is wider than the "Management Information" menu-area of ILSs such as INNOPAC, for example.

Traditionally, of course, the editorial scope of *The Acquisitions Librarian* has often been broader than "just Acquisitions." Witness Number 8 of *TAL: Popular Culture and Acquisitions*, which presents an integrated collection management/collection development/acquisitions approach. *TAL* Number 6: *Evaluation, Acquisitions, and Collection Management* also manifests this broad and "deep" approach to Acquisitions.

ACQUISITIONS AS OBTAINING EVERYTHING

Of course, Acquisitions is not now "just Acquisitions," nor has it ever really been "just Acquisitions"–at least in my opinion and experience! Increasingly libraries, and thus their Acquisitions Librarians, acquire copyright access, copy cataloging, management information reporting, assorted data sets, A/V items, in addition to the classic,

William E. Jarvis, Librarian 3 (Associate Professor level), is Collection Services Librarian, Washington State University Libraries, Pullman, WA 99164-5610 (e-mail: jarvis@wsu.edu).

[Haworth co-indexing entry note]: "Acquiring Online Management Reports: An Editorial Introduction." Jarvis, William E. Co-published simultaneously in *The Acquisitions Librarian* (The Haworth Information Press, an imprint of The Haworth Press, Inc.) No. 24, 2000, pp. 1-4; and: *Acquiring Online Management Reports* (ed: William E. Jarvis) The Haworth Information Press, an imprint of The Haworth Press, Inc., 2000, pp. 1-4. Single or multiple copies of this article are available for a fee from The Haworth Document Delivery Service [1-800-342-9678, 9:00 a.m. - 5:00 p.m. (EST). E-mail address: getinfo@haworthpressinc.com].

physically resident, manually retrievable print book and journal materials. Today, more than ever, Acquisitions is a McLuhanesque "mixed media" experience.

In regard to reports (and executive-type summaries, "decision-support" data) Acquisitions Librarians have always been acquiring/crafting/compiling management reports, both "narrow acquisitions" ones (funds, number of orders) and the broader comparative collection management reports, too. Now the opportunities available from online integrated systems and a variety of "external online system" sources make the tasks of acquiring online management reports a growing area. It's curious that report writer features are valued enough to be usually "RFPed," but it seems rare for any one vendor's ILS to be ruled out of a library's selection process primarily on the basis of its "reportology" features, although one always hears the constant lament of inadequate report features on just about any installed ILS.

Whether it's a circulation user report or a LC class range volume count, "yet to pay this year" order record survey, or a fund balance report hierarchy, the librarian must *acquire* the report, canned or ad hoc, turnkey or custom-built. *Acquiring Online Management Reports* is inevitably a "big tent" topic. Thus the varied contributions published here clearly demonstrate the vast opportunities and challenges before us in acquiring online management reports of all sorts, "acquisitions-module-specific" and otherwise.

"All management information reports," including "acquisitions reporting," "collection development reporting," and "collection management reporting" are closely associated endeavors. These functions overlap and have no absolute boundaries. In fact it is increasingly common for an ILS's overall management information features to be utilized in a trans-module fashion in one single report. Indeed, a system might routinely require a trans-modular use of bibliographic record fields, such as using a title field code, merely to alpha-sort a list of order records within an Acquisitions module. The demands of ILS management report acquisition are second order ones, as well as being trans-modular, system-wide in scope. The management reporter must be a professional with an adequate grasp of not only general report-generating features and necessary search logic but also of the detailed codes of many modules, templates, and system-record types in order to extract needed report data and formatting from within an ILS.

JUST EXACTLY WHAT ARE THEY?

Readers will note that I have not yet defined "online management reports" here. The empirical/operational definitions found in this volume's contributions are of course useful in that they operationally define online management reporting. However, for those more comfortable with definitive, explicit definitions, let me offer the following one of my own for "online management reporting": "The process of acquiring from online systems highly formatted and arranged data, citation lists, and/or other comparative information in order to compile, coordinate, understand, and manage both the online system, and all other related library processes." For users of Innovative Interfaces' ILS any of the results obtainable from the "Management Information" module, all of the submenu selections bundled together there can be considered "online management reports." Almost anything derived from an online source that is of use to a library manager can be called a management report.

VENDERS' ONLINE REPORTING SYSTEMS

This Number of *TAL* includes articles about various vendors' systems, several featuring vendor representatives as authors. Vendors' online reporting systems have a very long history, and for many libraries vendors' reports (such as three year historical serial price studies) predated any significant experience with "internal" integrated library systems, and indeed predate OPACs.

In the Internet-era, there has of course been an increase in the number both of online available *and* also in the quality of such materials vendor-operated systems. This collection is a "snapshot" of the state of the online management reporting art.

ON THE ARRANGEMENT OF THE PAPERS
IN THIS VOLUME

Here are some "housekeeping" points (and some philosophic context, too): With the exception of this editorial "Introduction" and my concluding "Coordinating Report Functions from Online Systems" essay, all contributions to this number have been arranged alphabetically by author. There are several reasons for this. It's a bit easier doing the editorial preparation this way of course, but more important- ly, there is little value here, in attempting to divide up these papers into a subtopic-subject type table of contents, given the multiplicity of the points touched on in a number of them. Not only are these individual contributions multi-faceted, of course–the whole collection samples the wide gamut of existing (or emerging) online report features. The theme of this *TAL* Number goes against the grain of a rigidly compart- mentalized view of management information reports. Although many of the contributors treat traditional acquisitions-type report functions in their studies, I do wish to stress the more universal applicability of the "reportology" dynamics dealt with here. There will be more about such fundamentals in my essay at the end of this volume.

LESS IS INDEED LESS

Finally, I need to point out that the "do more and more with less and less" philosophy and practice in US libraries has seriously constrained the development and analysis of library online management report processes and opportunities in a negative way. It has obviously im- pacted the implementation and maintenance of overall ILS/OPAC and Internet use and interpretation as well. This era of downsizing has negatively affected the availability of library professionals to contrib- ute their expertise to even "normal" library science–let alone to effect paradigm-shifts in library systems usage and service practices. The professional utilization of ILS and Internet management report writer software features clearly could benefit far more than currently feasible with the short-handed situation in most US libraries today.

Let me know what you think about this volume, and about what we can do to get good, useful online reports!

Will Jarvis

Serials Management Information
for the 21st Century

Amira Aaron
Ian M. Best

SUMMARY. This article discusses the value of management reports produced by serials vendors using state-of-the-art business systems. It describes a dedicated project by the Faxon Company, a member of the Dawson Information Services Group, to design and produce two series of collection development and financial reports from its recently developed business system, using input provided by the client community. New reporting capabilities from a sophisticated electronic information delivery system, Information Quest, are also discussed. Examples of these reports are provided. Collection development, acquisitions and serials librarians are urged to examine the benefits of vendor reporting and to continually provide input into the enhancement of currently available data and the development of creative new management reports required for today's library environments. *[Article copies available for a fee from The Haworth Document Delivery Service: 1-800-342-9678. E-mail address: <getinfo@haworthpressinc.com> Website: <http://www.haworthpressinc.com>]*

KEYWORDS. Online reports, business, Faxon, serials, vendors, Dawson

Amira Aaron, MLS, is Director of Academic Services at the Faxon Company (aaron@faxon.com). Ian M. Best is Chief Information Officer, Faxon Company, 15 Southwest Park, Westwood, MA 02090-1585 (best@faxon.com).

The authors would like to acknowledge the significant work done at Faxon by Adrian Alexander, then Senior Manager, Strategic Development, and David Fritsch, Director of Business Development, leading to the design and development of the report series described in this article.

[Haworth co-indexing entry note]: "Serials Management Information for the 21st Century." Aaron, Amira, and Ian M. Best. Co-published simultaneously in *The Acquisitions Librarian* (The Haworth Information Press, an imprint of The Haworth Press, Inc.) No. 24, 2000, pp. 5-20; and: *Acquiring Online Management Reports* (ed: William E. Jarvis) The Haworth Information Press, an imprint of The Haworth Press, Inc., 2000, pp. 5-20. Single or multiple copies of this article are available for a fee from The Haworth Document Delivery Service [1-800-342-9678, 9:00 a.m. - 5:00 p.m. (EST). E-mail address: getinfo@ haworthpressinc.com].

5

INTRODUCTION

Management reporting and analysis in the business of serials has become increasingly important in this era of budget reductions and transition to online access to journal literature. As the information and statistical needs of the client communities, both libraries and publishers, become more demanding and granular in nature, the reporting capabilities of modern vendor systems are being developed to provide added value to subscription services and aggregated electronic information delivery.

Serials vendors are able to provide varying levels of management information which transcend the local library collection. What follows are some observations about the value of vendor management information and descriptions of specific types of reporting developed by the Faxon and Dawson companies, as well as strong encouragement for continued input from the library and publisher communities.

LIBRARY AND PUBLISHER MANAGEMENT INFORMATION NEEDS

Serials and acquisitions librarians today need to closely monitor expenditures of both print and online serial collections. Price histories and projections sorted in a variety of ways are vital to their budget management efforts. Identification of unknown titles can often be achieved with the availability of membership/combination inclusion data. Recently, there has been a great need for assistance in identifying electronic titles that are available to the library at no additional charge as a result of the print subscription, or those that are entirely free of charge for a certain period of time.

Generally, collection development librarians are interested in two major capabilities: the need for detailed price information on serials within subject areas to create and justify allocation formulas and the results of the application of those formulas. A second need is the ability to evaluate the appropriateness and validity of the selections made of serials titles for specific collections, and a basis upon which to expand or contract the size of these collections. To accomplish these goals, librarians need to be able to compare the lists of titles they are receiving in a given subject area against different kinds of "authority lists."

Traditionally, publishers need to receive information about claim and order activity for titles, categories of purchasers, library budgets, and more. New demands by public service and collection development librarians, as well as publishers, are more sophisticated and detailed in nature. Data is needed about the online access patterns of researchers and end users to articles and tables of contents of journal literature which aggregated electronic information delivery systems are beginning to provide. Statistical reports of categorizations of users, titles accessed, selection of delivery options, and specific online behavior are becoming increasingly more in demand.

WHAT VENDORS CAN PROVIDE

Vendor databases generally contain a "universe" of serials information against which a library's own collection can be measured. In addition, price histories and projections are often available online in the vendor's business system. Some vendors have added value to their databases with the inclusion of standard subject codes and classifications, indexing and abstracting codes, language and country codes, and much more. Vendors with modern database systems are able to use powerful new database query tools to extract detailed and summary information as needed and present tailored reports to their clients.

Several vendors offer reports in a variety of formats, both print and electronic, for local manipulation. Obviously, management reports are more useful if the majority of a library's titles are placed with the same vendor. Pricing data is dependent on timely receipt from the vendor's suppliers, and the timing of production of pricing reports can be important in the correct interpretation of results.

Vendors who offer aggregated electronic content delivery and access systems are developing capabilities to provide the requisite user search information to both library managers and publishers. Document delivery and pay-per-view information is especially important to a library in evaluating the placement or cancellation of journal title subscriptions.

DEVELOPMENT OF FAXON'S REPORTING CAPABILITIES

Serials analysis capability, such as it exists, was largely the invention of the Faxon Company. Back in the 1970s, Faxon created a series of reports that, for the first time, gave collection development specialists quantitative analysis of serials without manual compilation of the numbers.

In later years, it became apparent that an urgent need existed for much more detailed reports and analyses of serials and serials collections. The pressure on library budgets caused by the serials crisis resulted in the need for better collection analysis tools for use by collection development and serials staffs. Most of the analysis tools that existed at that time were designed for the book collection, leaving a void in the area of serials.

In the early to mid 1990s, Faxon invested heavily in the development of a new state-of-the-art business system. In addition to being Year-2000 compliant, Faxon's business system offers great flexibility in generating documents and reports that efficiently address the needs of its clients today and into the future. The well-structured relational database design, coupled with the use of the powerful Impromptu® database query software from Cognos, allowed Faxon to pursue the creation of two important series of collection development and financial analysis reports for its serials subscription clients.

Intensive efforts on the part of Faxon's business development and information technology staff, working with input from major clients and collection development advisory groups, resulted in the new FELIX (Faxon Electronic Library Information Exchange) collection development report series and the SCOPE (Subject Classification of Periodicals) three-year serials price history and analysis service. Reports in both series can be produced on paper or in an ASCII delimited format so that clients can manipulate the data in their own chosen environment.

FELIX COLLECTION DEVELOPMENT REPORT SERIES

The FELIX collection development series of reports was developed for collection development librarians and other library managers, to help them more easily manage, evaluate and assess their entire serials collection. Specifically, Felix was designed to enable clients to maximize their effectiveness when making critical journal selection decisions, analyze their library's collection against the universe of serials in the Faxon database, project future costs more accurately and head off funding shortfalls, and to gain better control of their budget and renewal processes. New reports are added on a regular basis, many times as a result of client requests and discussions with collection development staff.

The following are descriptions of several of the more popular FE-LIX reports which we are asked to provide to our clients.

Inflation Projection Report

This report sorts a library's subscription list into the same categories as Faxon's "Subscription Price Projections" which are issued in February, April, and June of each year. The report then applies the projected differential inflation rates to each set of titles, and gives the client an approximation of what the total projected amount for the titles on the library's Faxon account will be by the end of the coming subscription year.

Abstract and Index Reports

One version of the abstract and index report sorts a client's list alphabetically by title, and indicates by which services the title is indexed and abstracted. The other report is sorted by the indexing/abstracting source and lists the client's titles under each source (see Figure 1).

Country of Origin Reports

One report sorts a client's titles alphabetically within the country of origin group. Collection managers can use this report to analyze their library's coverage by country or geographical region. A second report shows the universe of titles available through Faxon from any or all countries. Collection managers can use this report to compare their title selections from a given country or region to the Faxon Catalog's listings. They can then measure the breadth of their coverage and the financial exposure of such coverage.

Library of Congress Class Code (LCC) Reports

This report breaks out a client's list of titles by the two-character Library of Congress Class Code, then sorts each group into alphabetical order, and calculates the number of subscriptions and orders, and total expenditures, within each LCC. This report gives the collection

FIGURE 1

Faxon Collection Development Report Series	Abstract & Index Report by Title Client Name: Sample Client				
Title	Sub ID	Order Period	Total Amt w/o Svc Chg	AI Code	Abstract & Indexing Name
Adhesives age.	739197	01– April–1998 to 31 – March– 1999	$57.00	EN CA ST	Comendex Plus Chemical Abstracts Applied Science & Technology Index
Advances in polymer science	739199	Last part recvd: Polymer synthesis	$727.62	SC CA BA	Science Citation Index Chemical Abstracts Biological Abstracts
Advances in polymer technology	739200	01-Jan-1998 to 31-Dec-1998	$653.00	EN CA	Comendex Plus Chemical Abstracts
American Chemical Society Journal	13787972	01-Jan-1998 to 31-Dec-1998	$1,870.00	IM SC ST BA CA	Index Medicus Science Citation Index Applied Science & Technology Index Biological Abstracts Chemical Abstracts
Angewandte chemie. International edition. With Chemistry	42099523	01-Jan-1998 to 31-Dec-1998	$0.00	IM IC SC EN BA CA	Index Medicus Index Chemicus Science Citation Index Comendex Plus Biological Abstracts Chemical Abstracts
Angewandte makro-molekulare chemie.	12740412	01-Jan-1998 to 31-Dec-1998	$1,197.00	SC CA	Science Citation Index Chemical Abstracts
Appllied spectroscopy	739203	01-Jan-1998 to 31-Dec-1998	$290.00	EN BA	Comendex Plus Biological Abstracts

manager (especially one whose library uses LC classification for its serials) a complete profile of the collection. A second report provides the same breakdown, but also shows how many titles there are, according to the Faxon Catalog, within each LCC. The report also totals the cost of one copy of each title within each LCC. Collection managers seeking support for acquisitions funding and allocations can use this report to indicate weak or under-supported areas of the collection, and to develop allocations by subject on a fair and objective basis.

There are two additional reports that are exactly the same as those above, except that they use the entire LC call number from the MARC record rather than the two-character LCC.

North American Title Count (NATC) Reports

This report uses the North American Title Count (see Figure 2) categories as the grouping mechanism for titles. NATC is a collection development project, developed by ALA's Association for Library Collections and Technical Services (ALCTS), for large research libraries that began some years ago. The NATC methodology groups LC call numbers into "ranges" or "categories." For example, the call numbers AM1 through AM9999 are grouped into a range called "Museum Collectors and Collecting." NATC was originally developed for measuring the strength of book collections and comparing collections of peer institutions within the same call number ranges. Faxon now makes this methodology available for serials.

One NATC report enables a library to sort its own serial subscriptions using the NATC call number ranges. A second report allows a library to receive a complete list of serials from the Faxon databases in selected NATC call number ranges and indicates which of these titles are already part of the library's collection. The report can then be used for analyzing sections of the collection to determine where greater depth is needed and which additional titles may be appropriate for purchase. Summary and detail reports are available.

Titles by Supplier/Publisher Reports

These reports list titles alphabetically within publisher or supplier (generally the same as "publisher" except for fulfillment agents such as Neodata and other distributors). Collection managers can use the publisher/supplier reports to measure their financial exposure to specific publishers or to determine which titles they buy in order to evaluate eligibility for a consortium, for example. An additional report shows all titles in the Faxon catalog from up to three selected suppliers, indicating which of these titles the client has ordered.

FIGURE 2

Faxon Collection Development Report Series	North American Title Count Summary Client Name: Sample Client				
Call No. Range	NATC Category	Titles	Price	Ordered Titles	Expenditure
AC1-AC9999	Collections	2	$113.00	0	
AE1-AE9999	Encyclopedias	1	$44.05	0	
AG1-AG9999	General Reference Works	3	$216.38	1	$130.00
AI1-AI9999	Indexes	26	$27,785.53	2	$1,328.50
AM1-AM9999	Museums, Collectors & Collecting	16	$1,316.17	0	
AN1-AN9999	Newspapers (if used by campus)	150	$57,810.42	13	$4,973.15
AP1-AP9999	Periodicals	403	$34,243.87	19	$1,014.73
AS1-AS9999	Societies, Academies	123	$14,075.30	12	$646.42
AY1-AY9999	Yearbooks, Almanacs, Directories	1	$70.00	0	
AZ1-AZ9999	History of the Sciences in General, Scholarship, Learning	1	$30.00	0	
B1-B68	Philosophy: Periodicals, Societies, Congresses	95	$9,326.19	0	
B69-B789	Philosophy: History and Systems, Ancient through Renaissance	11	$739.06	0	
B790-B5739	Philosophy: History and Systems, Post Renaissance	26	$2,818.69	0	
BC1-BC9999	Logic	6	$1,336.50	0	
BD1-BD9999	Speculative Philosophy	8	$817.50	0	
BF1-BF1000	Psychology	214	$76,525.30	4	$942.50
BF1001-BF1400	Parapsychology	12	$737.47	0	
BF1401-BF19999	Occult Sciences	4	$60.50	0	
BH1-BH9999	Aesthetics	4	$269.02	0	
BJ1-BJ1800	Ethics	9	$633.30	1	$52.00
BL1-BL9999	Religions, Mythology, Rationalism	62	$3,699.60	0	
BM1-BM9999	Judaism	25	$973.25	0	
BP1-BP9999	Islam, Bahaism, Theosophy	24	$914.08	0	
BQ1-BQ9999	Buddhism	9	$320.82	0	
BR1-BR9999	Christianity (General)	125	$5,834.48	0	
BS1-BS9999	Bible	39	$2,406.80	0	
BT1-BT9999	Doctrinal Theology	10	$382.95	0	
BV1-BV9999	Practical Theology	83	$2,470.90	0	

Client Titles Available in Electronic Format

Our most frequently-requested of the FELIX series, this report compares a client's list of print titles to Faxon's database of journals available in electronic format. Clients use this report to quickly identify electronic journals which may be free of charge to them (or have a small fee attached) based on their print subscriptions. For the electronic journals, buying/licensing terms are also shown (see Figure 3).

Free Electronic Journals Available Through Faxon

This important report lists the electronic journals available through Faxon that are either free or free with a print subscription. It allows a client to identify free electronic titles quickly and easily, and provides vital online access information as well as print subscription costs.

Titles by Language Reports

One report lists a client's titles alphabetically within language of publication. The second report shows all of the titles in the Faxon database published in a given language.

Report of Memberships/Combinations/Inclusions

The first report lists all of a client's orders that represent membership or combination titles, along with the inclusion titles that are distributed with each one. A second report lists titles obtained as inclusions and shows the related membership or combination order. An additional report lists all titles to which a client subscribes individually that could be obtained as part of a combination or membership (see Figure 4).

Alphabetical List of Titles

This report lists alphabetically all of the client's titles ordered through Faxon–regular titles, inclusion titles, and combination or membership titles. For inclusion titles, the combination or membership title (i.e., the ordered title) is shown in the last column.

Brandon/Hill Titles for Medical Libraries

Published by the Medical Library Association, the Brandon/Hill lists are bibliographies of serials titles recommended for medical libraries. One FELIX report lists all of the titles recommended for small medical libraries and compares the list to titles available through Fax-

FIGURE 3

Faxon Collection Development Report Series	Client Titles Available in Electronic Format
	Client Name: Sample Client

Current Order Information	Electronic Journal Information
American Chemical Society Journal Sub ID: 13787972 Quantity: 1 Order period: 01-Jan-1998 to 31-Dec-1998 Catalog ID: 183416 ISSN: 00027863 Supplier: 544941 American Chemical Society URL: http://www.org/journals/jacesat/index.html	*Journal of the American Chemical Society* Cost: $19.58 for online 1 class C sub Comments: Print & online - 1 class C subnet is $22.38, site license only $3091.00
Analytical Chemistry Sub ID: 40002371 Quantity: 1 Order period: 01-Jan-1998 to 31-Dec-1998 Catalog ID: 140330 ISSN: 00032700 Supplier: 544941 American Chemical Society URL: http://www.org/journals/ancham/index.html	*Analytical Chemistry (full)* Cost: $851.00 for online 1 class C Comments: Print & online-1 class C subnet is $972.00, site license only $1343.00
Industrial & Engineering Chemistry Research Sub ID: 62022457 Quantity: 1 Order period: 01-Jan-19998 to 31-Dec-1998 Catalog ID: 48391299 ISSN: 08885885 Supplier: 544941 American Chemical Society URL: http://www.org/journals/iecred/index.html	*Industrial & Engineering Chemistry Research* Cost:: $972.00 for online C Comments: Print & online - 1 class C subnet is $111.00 site license only $1535.00
Inorganic Chemistry Sub ID: 63071043 Quantity: 1 Order period: 01-Jan-1998 to 31-Dec-1998 Catalog ID: 211281 ISSN: 00201669 Supplier: 544941 American Chemical Society URL: http://www.org/journals/inocajfindex.html	*Inorganic Chemistry* Cost: $1,612.00 for online 1 class C sub Comments: Print & online - 1 class C subnet is $1842.00 site license only $2544.00
Macromolecules Sub ID: 14836548 Quantity: 1 Order period: 01-Jan-1998 to 31-Dec-1998 Catalog ID: 117874 ISSN: 00249297 Supplier: 544941 American Chemical Society URL: http://www.org/journals/mamobx/index.html	*Macromolecules* Cost: $1617.00 for online 1 class C sub Comments: Print & online - 1 class C subnet is $1848.00 site license only $2553.00
Organometallics Sub ID: 16933700 Quantity: 1 Order period: 01-Jan-1998 to 31-Dec-1998 Catalog ID: 120992 ISSN: 02767333 Supplier: 544941 American Chemical Society URL: http://www.org/journals/orgnd7/index.html	*Organometallics* Cost: $1519.00 for online 1 class C sub Comments: Print & online - 1 class C subnet is $1736.00 site license only $2398.00
Science (AAAS) Sub ID: 739342 Quantity: 1 Order period: 01-Jan-1998 to 31-Dec-1998 Catalog ID: 113791 ISSN: 00368075 Supplier: 543884 AmerAssnforAdvScience URL: http://www.sciencemag.org/	*Science (AAAS)* Cost: see comments Comments: Online cost add'l $12.00 for indiv. memb, avail to non-members fall/97.

FIGURE 4

Faxon Collection Development Report Series	Membership/Combination Report Client Name: Sample Client List id: 1010160		
Membership/Combination Title	Memb/Comb ID	Inclusion Title	Inclusion ID
Academy of Accounting Historians, Membership	207113	The Accounting historians journal. Accounting historians notebook.	4734273 251259
ACI materials journal, With ACI structural journal and Concrete International.	240557	ACI materials journal	220981
		ACI strucutural journal. Concrete International, Design & construction	222430 213786
Advertising age.	118840	Ad age international Advertising age.	30565519 66217141
American Association for Artificial Intelligence, Membership Academic/corporate library subscription	245237	The AI directory	52585570
		AI magazine.	50488418
American Brahms Society Membership	186402	American Brahms Society Newsletter	252160
American Dialect Society, Membership	188639	American Dialect Society, Newsletter. American Dialect Society, Publications. American speech (American Dialect Society)	252326 252645 200734
The American economic review, With Journal of economic literature. With the Journal of economic perspectives	244783	American Economic Association, Survey of members. The American economic review. Journal of economic literature Journal of economic perspectives.	213716 250762 20079356 251612
American Fisheries Society, Library subscription, Including Transactions (Paper edition)	220239	Fisheries.	192995
		Journal of aquatic animal health, Insitutional subscription North American journal of fisheries management. Member rate. Additional copy only. The Progressive fish-culturist. Transactions of the American Fisheries Society.	251413 210267 32662560 11691104
American historical review, Class II subscription	215774	American Historical Association, Annual Report. American Historical Association, Program of the annual meeting.	210789 229871

on. Another report lists all of the titles recommended in the area of Allied Health and compares the list to titles available through Faxon. These reports allow the clients to measure the strength of their medical collections against the Brandon/Hill lists and help to identify weak or under-supported areas in their collections.

HISTORICAL PRICE ANALYSIS (SCOPE) REPORTS

These reports allow clients to compare the prices paid for their subscriptions over a period of three years. Each report lists all of the client's currently active Faxon orders where at least one subscription period has been priced. (Note that standing orders are not included.) Each entry displays:

- Title name
- Subscription ID
- The quantity ordered and the price paid (excluding service charge) for each of the past three years.
- Percentage increase or decrease in price for the current and past year.

For each primary sort field (except title), amounts are subtotaled, and total percentage increase/decrease from the previous year is computed. (A unit value is calculated for multiple-copy orders.) Grand totals are computed only for the Titles report. Clients may choose from a number of sort options. Within each primary sort, clients may choose to have the titles listed alphabetically, or in descending order by the latest price.

Sort options for SCOPE reports:
- Library of Congress Classification Code
- Call Number (Full LCC)
- Country of origin
- Language
- Currency (sorted by currency, but values shown in US dollars)
- Fund code (see Figure 5)

Note: Three separate fields (levels) are available in Source for fund codes. The report may be requested for any single level, for all three together, or for 1 and 2 combined. Note that the Source fund code fields may also be used by clients to store other types of information, such as subject headings.
- Ship-to (by Ship-to full address ID, or alphabetical by Mailstop)
- Publisher (alphabetical by publisher name)
- North American Title Count (see Figure 6)
- Format
- Titles only (alphabetically or by price)

FIGURE 5

Price History Sorted by Price Within Fund
Sample Client

Title Name	Sub ID	Qty	1998 Amount	% Inc	Qty	1997 Amount	% Inc	Qty	1996 Amount
Fund: ANSCF/ANNENBERG/ANSC									
• Media culture and society	22797	1	$240.00	20.00	1	$200.00	13.64	1	$176.00
• European journal of communication	21188	1	$216.00	12.50	1	$192.00	9.09	1	$176.00
• Journal of mass media ethics	22296	1	$215.00	16.22	1	$185.00	12.12	1	$165.00
• Journal of media economics	22306	1	$160.00	14.29	1	$140.00	21.74	1	$115.00
• Canadian journal of communication	20433	1	$85.00	6.25	1	$80.00	6.67	1	$75.00
• Australian journal of communication	20176	1	$74.35	11.52	1	$66.67	38.90	1	$48.00
• Media asia	22796	1	$43.00	4.88	1	$41.00	13.89	1	$36.00
• Asian journal of communication	20124	1	$36.00		1	$36.00		1	$36.00
Totals for fund: ANSCF/ANNENBERG/ANSC		8	$1,069.35		8	$940.67		8	$827.00
Total % increase:				13.68%			13.74%		
Fund: ANSCF/COMM ARTS & SCI/CAAS									
• Communication research (Sage)	20670	1	$309.00	11.96	1	$276.00	8.24	1	$255.00
• Journal of speech, language and hearing research	22485	1	$245.00	6.52	1	$230.00	2.22	1	$225.00
• Human communication research	21572	1	$220.00	11.68	1	$197.00	10.06	1	$179.00
• Intermedia (England)	21705	1	$129.39	− 2.52	1	$132.74	14.23	1	$116.20
• Broadcasting & cable	20327	1	$129.00	10.26	1	$117.00		1	$117.00
• Journal of communication	22057	1	$115.00	21.05	1	$95.00	10.47	1	$86.00
• Topicator	24257	1	$115.00	4.55	1	$110.00		1	$110.00
• Communication education	20665	1	$105.00	5.00	1	$100.00	4.17	1	$96.00
• Communication monographs	20667	1	$105.00	5.00	1	$100.00	4.17	1	$96.00
• Communication theory	20672	1	$105.00	5.00	1	$100.00	11.11	1	$90.00

Total % increase is calculated by including only orders that were placed in consecutive years and calculating a unit value for multiple copy orders.

INFORMATION QUEST REPORTING

A brand new opportunity exists for the collection of management information from aggregated electronic information delivery systems. Reports can be designed for both the library managers and content providers/publishers charting the statistics of end user behavior and

FIGURE 6

Price History Sorted by Title Within NATC
Sample Client

Title Name	Sub ID	1998			1997			1996	
		Qty	Amount	% Inc	Qty	Amount	% Inc	Qty	Amount
AP1-AP999 Periodicals									
• American quarterly	24830	1	$75.00	8.70	1	$69.00	4.55	1	$66.00
• American scholar	25018	1	$30.00	33.33	2	$45.00	− 19.64	1	$28.00
• Annales: histoire, sciences, sociales	24834	1	$122.97	− 26.88	1	$168.17	30.19	1	$129.17
• Antioch review. With Index	24838	1	$58.00	20.83	1	$48.00		1	$48.00
• Nation (New York)	24949	1	$75.00	70.45	2	$88.00	− 24.14	1	$58.00
• The New York review of books	24954	1	$55.00	11.11	1	$49.50		1	$49.50
•Times literary supplement, without index-U.S. & Canada only.	25012	1	$127.00		1	$127.00		1	$127.00
Totals for AP1 - AP9999:		7	$542.97		9	$594.67		7	$505.67
Total % increase:				2.80%*			4.45%*		
AS1 - AS9999 Societies, Academies									
• Minerva: a review of science, policy, and learning	24948	1	$174.50	− 3.86	1	$181.50	34.44	1	$135.00
Totals for AS1-AS9999:		1	$174.50		1	$181.50		1	$135.00
Total % increase:				− 3.86			34.44		
B1-B68 Philosophy: Periodicals, Societies, Congresses									
• Journal of the history of ideas	24934	1	$57.00	7.55	1	$53.00	8.16	1	$49.00
• Mind; A quarterly review of philosophy	24947	1	$86.00	17.81	1	$73.00	7.35	1	$68.00
• The Journal of Philosophy	24926	1	$75.00		1	$75.00	15.38	1	$65.00
• The Philosophical review	24962	1	$54.00		1	$54.00		1	$54.00
Totals for B1-B68:		4	$272.00		4	$255.00		4	$236.00
Total % increase:				6.67			8.05		

*Total % increase is calculated by including only orders that were placed in consecutive years and calculating a unit value for multiple copy orders.

detailed levels of access to electronic content by categories of users. Certainly, the production of these statistical reports is one of the real value-added services that aggregators provide for both the user administrators and the publishers.

Information Quest (IQ), a product of the Dawson Information Services Group, is one such state-of-the-art electronic information access system which was created in response to the challenges librarians, publishers, and information managers face as they move into a new electronic environment. IQ provides integrated Web-based solutions of information delivery and management, and powerful one-stop access to a wide range of electronic and print content. Up to 30,000 new citations are added each week, and activity on the system is brisk. Statistics are collected automatically and produced on a regular basis or on request.

Sample reports being developed specifically for library managers and content providers by IQ include:

1. *Articles Purchased Report*–includes number of documents ordered by fax, by pay-per-view, by subscriber, transaction date, user organization and user country.
2. *Articles Accessed Report*–includes number of hits on the abstract and article detail screens, as well as user information.
3. *Table of Contents (TOC) Report*–includes volume and issue and number of hits on the table of contents, as well as user information.
4. *Current Awareness Reports*–includes number of tables of contents (by titles and topics) set up to be received automatically by the user, as part of the *IQ Alerts* current awareness service, whenever appropriate new content is added to the database.
5. *Publication Report*–includes number of hits on a title in the browse function.
6. *Publisher Report*–includes number of hits on a publisher in the browse function.

FUTURE DEVELOPMENT PARTNERSHIPS

As serial vendors seek to expand their influence in the electronic environment and continue the provision of value-added services to their client communities, both libraries and publishers, management reporting capabilities take on increased significance. In addition to traditional serials management data, new reporting options from online aggregator services will provide crucial information to the users and providers of information on a much more granular level. Intelligent agents will be used increasingly to measure a user's search behavior and pinpoint areas of interest. Concerns about confidentiality and privacy protection must be addressed by our community as well.

Users of management information need to work closely with vendors to develop reporting capabilities and design appropriate, useful documents in a variety of formats. We would urge our clients to be creative and to approach their serial vendors with requests for new reports or enhancements to existing reports. This input is very much appreciated; it leads to innovations which improve both the level of service provided by the vendor and the ability of the librarian/information manager to more effectively control their serials collection and manage the access to information in their own institutions. Indeed, management reporting is one area which requires a true development partnership between the client and the vendor.

Electronic Resources:
Exactly, What Is Online?

SUMMARY. Librarians choosing to offer periodicals via electronic resources encounter many factors which influence satisfaction with the project. The purpose of this paper is to bring to the reader's attention the frequently overlooked areas of accuracy of information, extent of coverage of a journal, and updating of the coverage. These primary concerns are given much less attention in the literature than are fees, licensing agreements, and equipment. The writer addresses the question: Exactly, what is online? A determination of which electronic resource meets collection development goals and objectives must include an evaluative analysis of online information. The starting point for such an analysis is to describe the level of quality required by local standards of excellence and that which will meet users' needs. The methodology in this study began with the development of a checklist itemizing typical journal contents and publication information. The list was marked as notes were made in a page-by-page comparison of current issues and recent volumes with a random sampling of titles online. Information Access Company's *Business ASAP* and *Academic ASAP*, EBSCO's *Academic 1000* and UMI's *ProQuest Direct®* were studied. Numerous areas to examine in a local analysis are discussed. Librarians should be aware that full text coverage may mean selective items are covered in full text. The review of titles covered should include a look at the quality and appropriateness of the titles for the local library. Searching for the largest number of titles provided on an electronic resource may lead one away from collection development policies which are just as im-

Jetta Carol Culpepper is a Special Programs Librarian, Associate Professor, Murray State University Libraries, Murray, KY 41071-0009 (e-mail: <jetta.culpepper@ murraystate.edu>).

[Haworth co-indexing entry note]: "Electronic Resources: Exactly, What Is Online?" Culpepper, Jetta Carol. Co-published simultaneously in *The Acquisitions Librarian* (The Haworth Information Press, an imprint of The Haworth Press, Inc.) No. 24, 2000, pp. 21-28; and: *Acquiring Online Management Reports* (ed: William E. Jarvis) The Haworth Information Press, an imprint of The Haworth Press, Inc., 2000, pp. 21-28. Single or multiple copies of this article are available for a fee from The Haworth Document Delivery Service [1-800-342-9678, 9:00 a.m. - 5:00 p.m. (EST). E-mail address: getinfo@haworthpressinc.com].

portant for new formats as they are for paper formats. *[Article copies available for a fee from The Haworth Document Delivery Service: 1-800-342-9678. E-mail address: <getinfo@haworthpressinc.com> Website: <http://www.haworthpressinc.com>]*

KEYWORDS. EBSCO ProQuest (Information Access Co.), online reports, UMI

In the Murray State University Libraries we undertook a project to select electronic resources to supply periodicals via Internet connections or CD-ROM files. The selection committee and reviewers regarded their primary task to be the determination of which electronic resources would best meet collection development goals and objectives. Patron desire for immediate access to information and the need to address weaknesses in holdings were important service and collection development matters prompting the study of electronic resources. The possibility of accessing additional national newspapers or research journals online was exciting, especially given the dwindling purchasing power of the library budget. Yearly budgetary battles and inflation in current subscriptions make difficult any noticeable increase in the subscription base. Before selecting an electronic resource with potential for significant impact on holdings and document delivery service, an informal analysis of each database being considered was needed. Committee members made comparisons by entering searches and choosing delivery options on each of the databases. Their observations and reactions were shared within the committee. Possible choices of databases to which subscriptions seemed feasible were Information Access Company's *Business ASAP* and *Academic ASAP*, EBSCO's *Academic 1000* and UMI's *ProQuest Direct®*. Prior to the initiation of the review process, all were known to be excellent in their own emphasis and easy accessibility to end-users.

Price, equipment requirements and access agreements were important and ultimately major factors in the final decision. As reviews progressed, however, other factors formed an interesting question, what is online? Companies supplied lists of titles which answered the question somewhat. Nevertheless, once a librarian began working with the databases, this question became more intriguing. The Collection Analysis Librarian made notes on the accuracy of information, coverage of a journal and updates of the coverage. The evaluation continued with the development of a checklist which included typical journal contents and publication information. A random selection of titles from the library's collection of printed journals was compared page-by-page, and frequently word-by-word, with the same issues and volumes entered on the databases. It was expected that this comparison would yield the best results as to extent of coverage and accuracy of information in the databases.

Librarians quickly noted that a cover-to-cover comparison of contents between the printed copies and the online version of periodicals is difficult. An online search brought contents up in random order. Those who ever had thoughts of browsing through their favorite titles via electronic access and employing the same reading habits used for printed copies are destined to be disappointed and forced to learn the many search options. Few library patrons may be bothered by this situation. Most are seeking specific information needed for limited projects.

It was also quickly noted that "full text" is defined by those building each database and is to some extent based on the merits of the items appearing in the printed copy. Librarians selecting electronic resources will avoid disappointments if they take time to consider the purpose of the database. Any subsequent alterations in purposes of the database or revised suggestions for its use must be included in the review. Titles included in a database may satisfy collection development policies, but the critical matters of coverage, indexing, accessing options, and document delivery options must be given full consideration.

UMI's *ProQuest Direct®* includes indexing for covers, inside and outside pages, and citations for just about everything in between the covers. It merits mentioning, however, that like other databases which offer a number of document delivery options, all are not available for each item cited in the database. Users may find that requesting printouts is the best delivery option for the particular title or article.

Librarians concerned with providing full text of journals online or canceling paper subscriptions thought to be completely duplicated by electronic access need to analyze the particular database.[1] For many reasons titles which companies intended to cover in full text or partially may eventually turn out to be covered by a few items from selected issues. One reason is that authors are not unilaterally in agreement that their published material should be made available by electronic access. When permission is not granted to reproduce published material electronically all possible suppliers are restricted, unless permission is granted selectively. These situations are entirely unpredictable. It seems correct to anticipate some authors will not allow their writing to be copied for electronic access. Special issues in volumes and inserts in issues are frequently not included in electronic files.

Reviewers comparing printed issues with databases discovered that when several levels of information are indicated as available for a citation, much can be learned about the database contents.[2] Verifying whether or not those options identified as accessible actually bring to the screen the abstract, text, page image or page plus graphics, etc., is a must in analyzing database contents and ease of use. The fact is these things are not always in the database. Such happenings may simply be errors in constructing the database or may be an indication that construction is underway. Either situation is frustrating until corrected.

Scholarly journals containing only articles in English and published with few graphics and little mathematics receive more extensive coverage. Once a publication steps across this narrow description into charts, graphs, pictures, editorials, columns, letters, advertisements, short articles, feature articles, etc., the coverage available for delivery to the user's screen changes. The inclusion of charts and graphs may vary with the complexity of their structure. When page image is an option then complexity of all graphics, illustrations, and mathematics is somewhat less of a problem. Readability of the magnification on the full page image occasionally causes another difficulty. A few easily entered changes may solve the problem. Articles containing foreign language characters or symbols not utilized in the English alphabet may contain omissions instead of this information on some databases. Specifically this refers to characters which cannot be reproduced by the English alphabet on typewriter and computer keyboards. Coverage of journals published in foreign languages was not evaluated in this research.

In comparing paper issues with databases, reviewers noted that items entered by retyping are more likely to have spelling errors and omissions than articles entered by any of several other means. Also, incorrect citations and mixed text of articles would seem to be likely problems. In this study, however, they were infrequently encountered. It was noted that occasionally references and bibliographies would be mixed in with the text of articles. Items in both types of lists were sometimes omitted. Writers' notes and references appearing at the bottom of the page in printed copies were rather consistently entered following the text.

Formatting on databases initially draws attention until end-users become accustomed to the medium. Text of poetry is sometimes wrapped forming straight text. One questions if comprehension of meaning could possibly become problematic along with the ease of readability. Those who build databases occasionally ignore paragraph-ing in printed copies. When that happens, indentions appear to be randomly inserted to break the flow of text. Also, format or appear-ance of the text suffers when paragraph headers are run into the pre-ceding paragraph or the related paragraph–either may temporarily confuse readers.

Short articles and essays are not necessarily included in some data-base files.[3] Exceptions are those clearly related to the theme of the issue. Letters from well known personalities in the discipline are occa-sionally included and letters relevant to the subject dealt with in the issue. Very few advertisements appear in database files. Announce-ments of particularly newsworthy messages to practitioners are good examples of ads included. Book reviews which may be the journal's point of primary interest for practitioners and teachers are not always covered fully.

The review of a database should include a study of the quality and appropriateness of the titles covered for the local library's needs. Searching for an extensive listing of titles may cause one to stray from periodical collection development policies and plans which are impor-tant. The checklist used in this study included questions for which the librarian estimated probable extent of usage the title would receive. Also, an indication as to whether the title was recreational or scholarly reading was recorded. Here more insight as to the usefulness of the journals online and the level of research possible is gained.

Further efforts required that companies' supplied lists of titles in-cluded in databases be scanned for the number of titles which fall into the categories of leisure reading materials, newsletters or bulletins. Large general databases may contain titles for several reading and age levels. Those are likely constructed to appeal to end-users with interests varying from the leisure reading level to practitioners and scholars in selected subjects.

In regard to the question pertaining to updating coverage, dates of the most recent issues included were indicators of lag time between publication dates and date available on the particular database. It is possible to search a title one day, then repeat the search for issues the next day and find updates. It stands to reason that all titles are not updated daily–rather that updating in the files occurs daily. CD-ROM databases are regularly updated locally with each shipment of disks.

Once there is an answer to the question of what is online?, another question follows and needs to be answered in the final selection process. Does the resource meet local requirements for accuracy? The structure for building and maintaining each database reviewed involves management to effect valid contents. Self-reporting accessing the contents is vital. Reliability and accurate copying of printed publications are primary in establishing worth of a database.[4] Researchers are becoming more dependent on electronic resources for published materials and are moving away from simply relying on them for citations. Errors in contents, whether reported by staff or by subscribers, are corrected by the databases reviewed.

Prior to selection decisions, a review of database reports and other options to generate statistical information on usage could prevent concerns in the future. Electronic resources offer subscriber institutions periodic reports. Those reflect such matters as number of sessions, number of retrievals, time under access per reporting period, time of day, day of session, and average time of sessions. A listing of periodicals retrieved may show some statistical analysis of the top number of retrievals. This portion of the total review should include a determination of deliverable formats available for reports. Local office management may require American Standard Code for Information Interchange (ASCII), postscript or spreadsheet ready data rather than a printed report.

It is a good idea to check into software which the subscriber can set up locally to generate statistics on CD-ROM resources. These reporting systems may yield different information. Examples may be statistics on specific station traffic and even the number of attempts to log on to the database. Studying statistical reports over time will reveal if adequate access points have been licensed and which stations are used. Such reports will be valuable additions to firsthand observations in mak-

ing local assessments of the usefulness and interest in an electronic resource.

In conclusion, each database under consideration serves well as an
indexing reference. Rather than searching separately the yearly volumes of printed indexes, a single search on these electronic databases
scans citations for all years covered. Limiting the search to a specific
time frame or a particular journal are additional options.

A second advantage is the feature which permits searching in natural language. End-users work with a less formal and a more contemporary format than the structured subject headings in printed indexes.

The third point about the indexing is that each of the databases
evaluated include citation to more published material in many periodicals than is generally indexed in printed indexes. The *ProQuest Di-
rect®* database is an excellent example of extensive indexing.

Original and database created abstracts offer end-users an immediate
glance into articles. This affords a quick determination as to whether
reading either the online version or printed copy is necessary. Reading/
scanning articles online gives library patrons introductory information on
subjects. Key words to be utilized in additional searches and identifica-
tions of specific interest within wide categories may be identified.

Individual end-users must decide how to incorporate periodicals
supplied via electronic access into their work. They are to be alerted
that some potential exist for errors in contents. Authors and lectures
must weigh the importance of verifying exact wording before quoting
a passage. If publishers, teachers grading papers or other potential
critics are likely to require exact quotations, then one must conclude
that the printed copy remains the authoritative source. That withstand-
ing, text online is sought by researchers who will catch typographical
errors and adjust to format changes. When quick searches of indexes
and scanning of articles fit requirements, periodicals on electronic
files are time-saving answers to the information need. Clearly, these
databases have potential to fill some portions of the researchers' need
for citations and information. To ensure that happens, librarians evaluating databases by using the methodology employed in this project are
likely to be confident that choices are appropriate. Chances that unknown features of the electronic resources will be brought to their
attention later should be reduced.

NOTES

1. Hawbaker, A. Craig and Cynthia K. Wagner, "Periodical ownership versus fulltext online access: A cost-benefit analysis," *Journal of Academic Librarianship*, v. 22, no. 2 (Mar. 96), p. 105-109.

2. Orenstein, Ruth M., " 'How full is full' revisited: A status report on searching full-text periodicals," *Database*, v. 16, no. 5 (Oct. 93), p. 14-23.

3. Grzeszkiewicz, Anna and A. Craig Hawbaker, "Investigating a full-text journal database: A case of detection," *Database*, v. 19, no. 6 (Dec. 96), p. 59-62.

4. Ojala, Marydee, "Online, past, present and future: Repetition, reinvention, or reincarnation?" *Online*, v. 21, no. 1 (Jan. 97), p. 63-66.

Watch Out and Listen:
Faculty Assess Electronic Resources

Jetta Carol Culpepper

SUMMARY. The purpose of this study is to critique management reports provided by electronic databases. This will be done by discussing three database reports, an electronic report prepared locally and a local faculty assessment. The latter was created to seek end-users' reactions. The database-produced reports are: OCLC's FirstSearch Usage Statistics Online, SilverPlatter's Electronic Reference Library software-generated reports and Information Access Company's SearchBank Usage Statistics. The fourth report was a record of the usage of only CD-ROM resources and was produced from the configuration of locally acquired software. Data from the fifth reporting method discussed, an assessment by faculty, is compared to that from the report-yielding features of the databases. Faculty in all disciplines offered at a regional university relied on their individual research experiences to provide information regarding the effectiveness of databases in filling the consumer's needs. While less than half of the faculty participated, questions designed to help assess research strategies, teaching methods and usefulness of specific databases provided much data. Analysis of the data collected electronically showed some remarkable similarities to faculty's self-reports of research and perceptions of students' research. Awareness of the electronic reports may increase the potential for faculty utilization of these resources in teaching and research. Contents of the electronic databases either parallel paper subscriptions or are additional titles supplying indexing, abstracting and full text of journals and newspapers.

Jetta Carol Culpepper is a Special Programs Librarian, Associate Professor, Murray State University Libraries, Murray, KY 42071-0009 (e-mail: <jetta.culpepper @murraystate.edu>).

[Haworth co-indexing entry note]: "Watch Out and Listen: Faculty Assess Electronic Resources." Culpepper, Jetta Carol. Co-published simultaneously in *The Acquisitions Librarian* (The Haworth Information Press, an imprint of The Haworth Press, Inc.) No. 24, 2000, pp. 29-40; and: *Acquiring Online Management Reports* (ed: William E. Jarvis) The Haworth Information Press, an imprint of The Haworth Press, Inc., 2000, pp. 29-40. Single or multiple copies of this article are available for a fee from The Haworth Document Delivery Service [1-800-342-9678, 9:00 a.m. - 5:00 p.m. (EST). E-mail address: getinfo@haworthpressinc. com].

29

Data showing interest levels in utilizing 22 electronic resources and their weaknesses in filling needs indicate strengths of the five reports as tools to direct management. Usefulness of the electronic reports is fully supported by the faculty assessment. *[Article copies available for a fee from The Haworth Document Delivery Service: 1-800-342-9678. E-mail address: <getinfo@haworthpressinc.com> Website: <http://www.haworthpressinc.com>]*

KEYWORDS. Electronic, OCLC, SilverPlatter (Information Access Co.), faculty assessment, online reports

The instrument used by faculty collected only evidence of the local impact caused by providing newly created electronic research resources and digitized paper formats. The meaning of the data was enhanced by turning to the literature on end-users' reactions to online research experiences. Points applicable to other institutions offering or considering electronic resources are given.

It was concluded that qualities of electronic resources and features of printed materials uniquely nurture the quest for information. In explaining that faculty are not abandoning all paper formatted resources, satisfaction with both research options is discussed. The report provided evidence of needs and sufficient justification for acquiring access to more carefully selected databases. Preference was for a general database complemented by subject specific resources. Comments of faculty discouraged management from financing additional electronic holdings by placing less emphasis on the acquisition of books and paper formatted periodicals in the future.

The objective of this study is to review management reports produced by electronic databases. That is partially achieved by comparing each with two other reports. The first is an electronic report produced locally. The second is a faculty assessment. Teaching faculty working in all disciplines at Murray State University, a regional university of 8,800 students and 375 faculty participated. The 22 databases evaluated are listed in the summary chart. Examples of useful information from electronic reports are given throughout the discussion for acquisitions librarians and other administrators.

The first management reports reviewed were OCLC's FirstSearch Usage Statistics Online. The reporting method generates individual authorization, institution and group level reports for three types of accounts:

The Per-search account has a specific number of searches allocated to an authorization or group of authorizations. Reports provide search information at the database level, total number of sessions and simultaneous user information.

The Subscription account has access to specific databases where searching is only limited by the number of simultaneous logons allowed. Reports provide total sessions, turnaways, port utilization (simultaneous logon information) and detailed search information.

The Hybrid account combines per-search and subscription database access under a single authorization or group of authorizations. Reports provide total sessions, turnaways, port utilization (simultaneous logon information) and detailed search information.

The usage statistics reports may include eight specific categories of information:

> total searches
> databases searched and number of searches for each database
> port utilization information (simultaneous user information)
> session turnaways
> database turnaways
> total number of authorizations used for an institution or group
> number of online full text documents retrieved
> total number of sessions.

These reports for monthly time frames are available via the Internet. Correct authorization and password are necessary for viewing data. The local administrator may change the password, navigate through reports and print reports for study and analysis. Local access to First-Search is accommodated through a consortium referred to as the Kentucky Library Network on the electronic reports. For the purposes of this study only institutional reports for Murray State University were analyzed.

The second set of reports reviewed were for SilverPlatter's products. Their Electronic Reference Library (ERL), a server software, prepared the statistical data. The program can be run on any client workstation. Upon configuring it to point to the ERL server, an administrator may use it to control which users will be allowed to access which databases. It also enables an administrator to gather statistics about users and databases that access the server. The factors included in the statistics for each product used are as follows:

amount of time the user is "connected" to the database
number of successful logins to the database
number of rejected logins
dates of the reported statistics
number of characters viewed
number of records browsed with the abstract field in the display
number of records browsed.

Information Access Company's SearchBank Usage Statistics were the third reports reviewed. They are delivered on a monthly basis via e-mail and can be configured to provide the following information:

total sessions
connect time
average session time
total views
total retrievals
monthly database usage
time of day/day of week
titles retrieved listed alphabetically or top number of retrievals.

These reports are available in American Standard Code for Information Interchange, PostScript or spreadsheet formats. Statistics are recorded for each library with a separate login or location id.

The fourth means of reporting was the use of locally acquired software. Technicians configured it to statistically record usage of CD-ROMs. Categories by which data was separated were very similar to those in typical database generated reports. This electronic means of gathering information probably permits the most leverage in the creation of statistical checks to address concerns. Reporting by the CD-ROM server may be more appropriate for other subscribers. There licensing metering software limits the number of simultaneous accesses and collects statistics. The online reports are handy resources which acquisition librarians and others will consult.

A review of monthly statements from each electronic source showed peak usage weeks. Statistics regarding logons and rejected logins revealed that the number of ports and workstations available were adequate. Lower usage times reported most frequently occurred during school holidays and when enrollment was dependent upon short term or summer curriculum. Lower enrollment during those times would be expected to produce lower usage statistics. Additional categories in the reports, when analyzed, both overlap features of the faculty assessment and are statistically similar. Most likely the strongest review which can be presented for administrators will be provided by referring to the faculty reporting. Only statistics from the faculty assessment will be included to demonstrate the usefulness of all reports.

This review of the fifth set of reports, the faculty assessment, could lead administrators to anticipate the possibilities for utilizing electronic reports are probably only limited by local creativity, resources through which to access databases and funding. The evaluation and response routine was primarily designed to determine if faculty considered particular resources helpful. Gaining insight into teaching methods and research strategies which may influence the need for electronic resources was a secondary goal. It was anticipated that the expedient and easiest way to gather data would be through worksheets constructed largely of check-off questions. Selected questions required single word responses. Faculty were given the option of submitting extensive written comments on the backsides of pages or appending any thoughts deemed worthy of input. Detailed instructions for making evaluations were not given. Evaluators were permitted to respond from previous experiences or to record evaluations as they worked with each resource. Those finding a resource useful in teaching or research marked "Yes." Resources not found to be helpful were marked "No." Items considered not to be relevant were marked "NR." Departmental affiliation of each evaluator was requested to facilitate association of responses with curriculum areas. Signatures on assessment reports were not necessary, since only members of the evaluating group were given an opportunity to participate. The curriculum and faculty expertise surely influenced responses. Results show it was insignificant that less than half of the total faculty voluntarily made assessments. Participation from across the curriculum brought forth an abundance of usable data.

Evaluations did not look into specific problems in using databases. Errors occurring as searches were input or search options yielding puzzling results were considered queries for a separate study.[1] Controlled vocabulary may have had an impact on end-users. Comments and observations on such detailed reactions are to be found in current writings.[2] Response time affecting attitudes favoring CD-ROMs or electronic connections to the home database was left for other researchers to weigh as they study web based service.[3] Faculty were not specifically queried as to their individual analysis of database construction. Those matters will surely be discussed at another time.

Sixty percent of the participants indicated they used electronic resources only three to four times a year. Those figures may be partially explained by statements that they occasionally used only the card catalog and paper indexes for their limited needs. A surprising 36% reported weekly usage of the electronic resources. Data collected showed that 81% found the combination of online, handouts, and staff instructions helpful. All of these statistics reveal that faculty are interested in electronic resources and receptive to incorporating the new format both into teaching and professional research. There is no specific indication as to exactly how the resources are utilized. Nevertheless, it is clear that faculty expect students to employ the new technology which they use. Research not involving reading lengthy articles at public computers is the more likely strategy. Patrons waiting in line would prefer that the reader turn to printed copies, e-mail the item to their personal computer or, find another means of delivery.[4] Numerous research options, ease of moving through documents and the several choices for delivery of selections allow for electronic resources to make a significant impact. During this transit time when the extent of electronic change is evolving, research strategies are changing in conformity.[5] Classroom teachers and librarians report including electronic resources in information literacy training which is necessary for learning throughout one's life.

ERIC was the only database under evaluation which was offered on CD-ROM and through FirstSearch. The higher percentage of faculty finding the CD-ROM product useful versus the percentage selecting the FirstSearch product is likely due to the fact that FirstSearch had been available for less time. Researchers introduced first to the CD-ROM version of *ERIC* had a much greater opportunity to work with it. Probably many of those users stayed with the CD-ROM version instead of switching back and forth between the two. Those evaluators may have felt more confident in their research strategies with the CD-ROM version. *ERIC* was assessed as the most helpful of the CD-ROM databases. The category for teaching was marked by 55% and the research category was marked by 68%. *The Humanities Index* was marked by 37% for teaching and by 43% for faculty research. The

Social Sciences Index was close in line with 33% using it in their teaching and 52% finding it applicable in their professional research. *ERIC*, the *Humanities Index* and the *Social Sciences Index* cover subjects appealing to a wide spectrum of users and would be expected to be assessed higher than subject area resources.

A characteristic of electronic resource utilization at this institution is evident in evaluations of the ever popular *Oxford English Dictionary*. The CD-ROM version was marked as applicable in teaching by 33% and useful in faculty research by 30%. Apparently, faculty using the databases were primarily seeking indexing, abstracting and/or text. Perhaps many students and faculty came to the library after getting an introduction to the subjects from other sources. In which case, spellings of research words and assistance in writing papers may not be as important as it would be for the unprepared researcher. Much assistance in finding key words to research and information on spelling is to be gained by entering searches on the appropriate database. Clearly, there is a need for the CD-ROM version of the dictionary. Student assessments would be much higher.

PsychLit, Art Abstracts, Applied Science and Technology Index, CINAHL, and *Biological and Agricultural Index* on CD-ROM were very favorably received by the subject areas. Percentages of the total faculty making reports ranged from 10%-23% in useful for teaching for these titles. Faculty researchers marked these resources from 10%-35% as useful. An interpretation of the data requires looking at each category checked in combination with written comments and enrollments in subject areas. Each resource is helpful in a portion of the academic programs. The lower numbers only represent the number of participants in those subject areas.

In the FirstSearch grouping, *Books in Print* received a 55% assessment as applicability to teaching. Seventy percent marked it as usefulness for faculty's research. Both statistics fell within the expected range, given the popularity of printed copies. Faculty regularly use this resource in compiling bibliographies. *ArticleFirst*, a general resource, was marked as helpful to teaching by 25%. Useful in professional research was checked by 33%. Other electronic resources in this group were marked from 3%-22% useful in teaching and 8%-22% useful in faculty research. This data drew an immediate response. Publicity materials and instructional sheets were mailed to departments identified as being the affiliation of these evaluators. Several faculty did not submit assessments for all of the resources. In some instances, the reason for not reporting many have been the unknown potential for use in an updating curriculum. It is anticipated that statistics on usefulness of all databases will increase as faculty become more acquainted with FirstSearch. Observations of student work indicate FirstSearch resources are constantly in use.

Information Access Company's InfoTrac titles are the electronic resources offered for the longest period of time. *Expanded Academic ASAP* was marked by 35% as applicable in teaching and 52% indicated it was useful in their research. *Business ASAP* was marked as applicable in teaching by 25% and useful in their professional research by 23%. Both resources are used frequently by faculty and students. Researchers from the business programs find *Business ASAP* especially helpful. The *National Newspaper Index* received a 40% marking for teaching uses and 38% for professional research. Titles indexed on this database are: *The New York Times, The Wall Street Journal, The Christian Science Monitor, The Washington Post* and *Los Angeles Times.* This resource provides information for many disciplines.

Faculty were asked if they could select more resources to support their teaching and research needs which formats would be most important. No limit was placed on the number of formats which could be marked or added to the list. Books were marked by 48%, audiovisuals by 28%, CD-ROMs by 40%, microfilm by 10%, periodicals by 75%, and online databases by 55%. These statistics clearly indicate that faculty are not abandoning printed formats. In addition, the majority of the evaluators desire more electronic research sources.

Library managers utilizing this data will not consider canceling subscriptions to finance online resources. Intentions, if there ever were any, to acquire future subscriptions only through electronic access are certain to meet opposition. Several of those faculty justified requests by mentioning problems encountered when the Interlibrary Loan Service reaches the maximum number of orders permitted. Evaluators in the health sciences, biology, chemistry, music and special education were particularly firm in emphasizing needs for both journals and electronic resources. According to comments submitted, these faculty, like many others, have research projects underway continually. Research is often a portion of their course requirements.

Preference was clearly for the general databases offered to be complemented by adding subject resources. Evaluators requested *AGRI-*

COLA and more resources like *MEDLINE.* Teachers in music requested an electronic database but did not name a particular one. A small number of faculty requesting *Current Contents* mentioned that they regard it as offering more information than similar databases already offered. Faculty stated a need for sufficient information on other writers to be able to contact them for copies of articles. The ability to access library catalogs of additional neighboring universities was requested. Evaluators expressed hoped that direct connections to library catalogs would supply needed information. Several mentioned intentions to travel to the universities owning the needed materials. Other faculty requested, "more electronic research resources," "more books," "more periodicals" and a few stated "more of everything." These comments may be reactions to slow growth in local collections. The only exception being the fairly recent leap forward into electronic resources. That growth necessitated this study of the usefulness of the resources.

The interest in printed materials may be explained by several factors. Perhaps the experience of having in hand the original printing of articles is important to readers. Printed journals can be carried around in the building and read along with books or other resources. Journal issues centered around a theme allow the user to quickly read/scan through the entire issue. Also, books retain their status as providers of information. Printed books may be checked out and carried anywhere the reader chooses. Established patterns for scanning and note taking may relate to a preference for printed copies. Finally, a factor of association and recall related to illustrations, graphics and mathematics on the printed page may influence some readers.

In summarizing findings for the faculty assessment, the majority of the evaluators found electronic resources relevant and helpful in their teaching and/or research. Data clearly points to both weak areas in holdings and the most useful resources. Statistics indicating the percentage of evaluators who found resources not applicable to either teaching or research ranged from very small for most resources to a moderate percentage for a few titles. Resources had been selected in anticipation that each would not be equally useful for all disciplines. It is apparent that the 22 electronic resources had been carefully chosen to meet information needs. The worksheets employed in guiding evaluations and collecting data met the purposes of the study well. Both statistics and comments indicated a definite need for more printed and electronic resources. Unique qualities of both formats meet needs for information.

In conclusion, the new electronic report yielding features reviewed produced OCLC's FirstSearch Usage Statistics Online, SilverPlatter's Electronic Reference Library software generated reports and Information Access Company's SearchBank Usage Statistics. A study of the contents of these reports, a locally generated electronic report and data collected in the faculty assessment clearly points to the utility of electronic reports. The faculty assessment report used in this study included specific personal assessments by end-users. A generalized analysis of the two reporting methods and comparison of each electronic report with the faculty assessment report revealed tremendous similarity in all statistics. Interpretation and study of the electronic reports generally lead to the same findings as were revealed in the faculty assessment. It seemed appropriate to include only one statistical summary for the reader. In this instance, the local assessment by faculty which produced possibly the strongest evidence of the validity and usability of electronic reports is offered.

Several viable electronic options for gathering statistics exist. Owners of electronic resources routinely design usage reports. Choice of delivery method is usually determined by the local administrator. New subscribers participating in consortia should be aware that reports may be directed to management of the consortia. Planning review structures before activating a subscription could avoid potential delays in data reaching local personnel.

Reporting by whatever option should include information on time connected per reporting period and number of times each resource was accessed. Some reporting methods will check for lapse time at established intervals and close the program when it is not in use. A particularly important statistic is the number of stations where end-users are waiting to access the program at a given time. Reports of the number of rejected accesses may flag logon errors and malfunctions of the system. A structure for reviewing electronic reports and following up where appropriate will surely yield more satisfaction for end-users. Arguments can clearly be made for not basing decisions to maintain or cancel subscriptions solely on electronic report data. Readers should, however, note their unmistakable importance in making management decisions.

NOTES

1. Diane DiMartino and Lucinda R. Zoe, "End-user full-text searching: Access or Excess?" *Library and Information Science Research*, v. 18, Spr. 1996, p. 138-140.

2. Marydee Ojala, "Troubleshooting your search: Whatever can go wrong, will go wrong," *Online*, v. 19, no. 6 (Nov. 95), p. 59-61.

3. Carol Tenopir, "Online databases," *Library Journal*, v. 121, Dec. 1996, p. 35-36.

4. Susanne Bjorner, "Cleaning up search results: What do we expect?" *Online*, v. 19, no. 3 (Mar. 95), p. 65.

5. Ann Schaffer, Neil Calkin, and Rita Echt, "Scholarly Journals at the Crossroads," *The Serials Librarian*, v. 28, no. 3/4, p. 356

PARTIAL STATISTICAL SUMMARY OF WORKSHEETS

For the resources listed below, faculty considering a resource useful in teaching or research marked "Yes." Resources not considered helpful were marked "No." Items considered not relevant were marked "NR."

CD-ROM RESOURCES	TEACHING			RESEARCH		
	Yes	No	NR	Yes	No	NR
PsycLit	22%	11%	47%	35%	8%	43%
Art Abst., App.Sci. & Tech.	23%	10%	62%	25%	46%	62%
Humanities Index	37%	6%	41%	43%	35%	40%
Nursing (CINAHL)	10%	10%	71%	10%	13%	63%
ERIC	55%	4%	27%	68%	6%	25%
Biolog. & Agri.	20%	10%	33%	20%	6%	43%
Social Sci. Index	33%	8%	40%	52%	11%	27%
Dictionary (Oxford Eng. Dict.)	33%	11%	32%	30%	10%	35%
FIRSTSEARCH RESOURCES						
WorldCat	22%	5%	28%	22%	6%	23%
ArticleFirst	25%	6%	28%	33%	6%	16%
ContentsFirst	20%	8%	27%	22%	5%	25%
FastDoc	17%	8%	22%	22%	8%	22%
NetFirst	13%	5%	23%	22%	3%	22%
Books in Print	55%	6%	20%	70%	3%	13%
EBSCO	3%	11%	40%	10%	23%	37%
ERIC	37%	3%	23%	55%	6%	15%
GPO	6%	11%	32%	8%	11%	32%
MEDLINE	17%	10%	32%	18%	20%	25%
MLA Bibliography	18%	11%	30%	18%	13%	32%
ProceedingsFirst	8%	10%	30%	15%	11%	27%
INFORMATION ACCESS COMPANY'S INFOTRAC						
Expanded Academic ASAP	35%	3%	28%	52%	10%	28%
Business ASAP	25%	13%	37%	23%	11%	38%
National Newspaper Index	40%	10%	25%	38%	11%	25%

Library Management Statistics from an Integrated Library System (ILS)

Jeannie H. Dixon

KEYWORDS. Reports, online, ILS

THE NEED FOR MANAGEMENT STATISTICS

Library management requires statistics to address a variety of issues, such as staffing needs, facility planning (space, hours of operation, capital needs), budget forecasting and fiscal management. Justification for increases in resources will include the appropriate statistics. The availability of accurate, current management data could mean the difference in having a request for additional staff or budget approved or denied.

The state and federal governments require management statistics for state and national data gathering activities for planning and comparison. The U.S. National Center for Education Statistics IPEDS (Integrated Postsecondary Education Data System) Academic Libraries survey collects and reports national data biennially and is used as a basis for some state-level surveys. Public library data is gathered annually by NCES (through the Federal-State Cooperative System) and by ALA-PLA (through the Public Library Data Service).

Jeannie H. Dixon is Assistant Director for Library Software Operations, College Center for Library Automation, Tallahassee, FL 32304 (e-mail: jeannie@ccla.lib.fl.us).

[Haworth co-indexing entry note]: "Library Management Statistics from an Integrated Library System (ILS)." Dixon, Jeannie H. Co-published simultaneously in *The Acquisitions Librarian* (The Haworth Information Press, an imprint of The Haworth Press, Inc.) No. 24, 2000, pp. 41-46; and: *Acquiring Online Management Reports* (ed: William E. Jarvis) The Haworth Information Press, an imprint of The Haworth Press, Inc., 2000, pp. 41-46. Single or multiple copies of this article are available for a fee from The Haworth Document Delivery Service [1-800-342-9678, 9:00 a.m. - 5:00 p.m. (EST). E-mail address: getinfo@haworthpressinc.com].

IDENTIFICATION OF NEEDED STATISTICS

Historically, statistics have been kept manually by staff or estimated through sampling. Manual statistics have problems in reliability and in cost-effectiveness. Sampling provides a way to reduce the costs of data gathering efforts and can be highly reliable. The ability of the automation software package to provide accurate and cost-effective statistics is a valuable feature. Many requests for bids for Integrated Library Systems (ILS) include the requirement for statistical reporting. For some libraries, the reports provided by the vendor provide all the required statistics. For other libraries, additional statistics are needed which must be provided by custom reports. By gathering all of the needed data elements, the library manager can then determine which statistics are generated by the ILS and which will need to be gathered by an alternate method.

It is important to realize that an ILS will never be able to provide all of the required statistics. For example, most state or national surveys ask questions relating to facility use. The ILS does not provide the information needed for the traditional door count numbers, but could provide numbers on circulation of the collection.

With an ILS, statistics may be derived from a variety of sources. The transaction log can be analyzed and data extracted for some statistics. The item and borrower files counter fields can be utilized to gather other statistics. The title database will yield even more data elements such as age, size, and degree of duplication in the collection. Some of the data may be cross-tabulated to give a more detailed description of the activity or resource being reported. This can quickly lead to a case of statistical overkill; too many sources for reporting similar data. For example, when a count of all materials circulated can be retrieved from several different reports, which provides the desired information in the format needed? Does the report on item circulation (which would provide collection activity) meet the need better than the agency circulation (which provides data on desk activity)?

CREATION OF STATISTICS PACKAGE

Using the information gathered in the analysis of required statistical data, the library manager can begin to identify the reports that provide the needed information. The manager will need to determine which statistics are not provided by the canned reports. If the library has a report-generating software package, reports can be created to provide this information.

Resources readily available can be utilized to gather data or to manipulate the data gathered by the report packages. System commands can be used together with programming languages or other available statistical packages to provide the information. In order to produce a report on the age of the business collection for an accreditation visit, FORTRAN can be utilized to extract data from the bibliographic database. Using that information, utilize SAS(r) to determine the median and mean age of the collection based on the publication dates of materials in specific call number ranges.

Once the base set of data elements and which reports generate the data is determined, it is important to document this information. The information to be documented should include what is being counted, the source of the count, and to whom and how often the information is distributed. For example, if the library board requires at its monthly meeting the total circulation count for the previous month, the documentation for the report would be similar to:

For:	Library board monthly meeting (second Tuesday each month)
What:	Total circulation count
Source:	Grand total from the monthly item circulation report for the month just ended
Frequency:	Every month the information needs to be provided to the director's secretary on the Friday before the board meeting

This will ensure that accurate statistics are provided on time and consistently. It will also ensure that each month the item circulation count is reported, not the borrower circulation count.

STATEWIDE STATISTICS–A CASE IN POINT

Florida's College Center for Library Automation (CCLA) is a statewide project providing library automation to the twenty-eight public community colleges of Florida, through LINCC, its automated network. Utilizing software from Data Research Associates (DRA), the system consists of a union bibliographic database, borrower database, and item file shared by the libraries. The ability to gather statistics with a statewide perspective is a strong feature of this system.

Monthly and annual statistics are produced and distributed to the libraries. A major project is underway to tie the statistics to the IPEDS and State Library reports. All reports produced by CCLA, both the canned reports provided by DRA and the custom reports written by CCLA staff, are documented in *LINCC Standard Reports*. Each report is given a unique number which is used to identify it in other statistical documents.

CCLA is developing a data element dictionary to define each element in the statistics package. The dictionary details the source of the data (giving the LINCC standard report number, where appropriate) and the frequency of the data gathering. Information on which state or national statistical survey utilizes this data will also be included.

This work began with an analysis of the IPEDS report and other survey tools in use in Florida by the community colleges. A review of existing CCLA reports indicated the source for much of the data. Data which was needed but not yet provided by existing reports was compiled. That information was reviewed to determine if it was appropriate for the system to provide the data, or if it was more appropriate for the individual library to keep the data. Additional reports were then created by CCLA staff to complete the package.

Our DRA system includes the circulation, cataloging, online catalog, acquisitions, and serials modules. At the implementation of the serials and acquisitions modules, CCLA staff reviewed the reports provided by DRA and developed additional custom reports. In the area of acquisitions, reports were developed to provide data on the number of orders placed, invoice activity, and fund activity. Custom reports such as vendor performance and average cost of materials purchased statewide through the online system are also possible.

In the area of serials management, custom reports included counts of the number of claims created, copy records created, and serial issues checked in.

The Florida State Board of Community Colleges is required by law to review instructional programs every five years. In 1996, a program review was conducted for the Library and Learning Resource Centers at the state's 28 community colleges. Part of this review utilized information from a collection assessment study using data gathered from LINCC by custom reports written by CCLA staff and analyzed by Anna Perrault and John DePew. The study reviewed the age of the collections in the statewide database, and found that 33% of the printed materials were published after 1980, 31% were published in the 1970s and 35% were published prior to 1970. This reveals that approximately 66% of the collections are more than 25 years old.

This information was cited in the program review, and it was recommended that funding be sought to replace at least 5% of the community college collection each year. The program review further recommended that non-recurring, supplemental funds be requested of the Legislature to update the current printed materials collection in the community colleges. The 1998-99 Legislative Budget Request for the State Board of Community Colleges therefore includes a request for $6,785,893. This amount was determined by the following formula:

current book holdings as of June 30, 1996 * 5% increase * $50.44 (2,674,739 * .05 * 50.44) = $6,785,893

The cost of $50.44 was taken from *Choice Study*, which lists the national average cost per book.

This is one example of how library management statistics are generated and utilized from an Integrated Library System. Regardless of the size of the library, or the ILS in use, the primary factor in utilizing the statistics is the consistency of extraction and the comparability of the figures. It is important that the statistics are documented as to their source to ensure consistent extraction and reporting. By defining the source of the data, it is possible to then compare the numbers to those of other libraries. This ensures that like statistics are compared and will aid in appropriate conclusions.

BRIEF BIBLIOGRAPHY

There are many articles on the use of statistics in libraries. The *Library Administration & Management* Winter 1996 issue has five articles under the heading "Mining your automated system for better management." Walt Crawford's *Library Hi Tech* article on numeracy is particularly good for putting the whole statistics picture into proper focus. The National Information Standards Organization has published the 1995 revision of the ANSI standard Z39.7 for library statistics which contains valuable information and sources for use in compiling state and national statistics.

REFERENCES

Choice Study. U.S. Book Prices January-December 1996. March 1997.

Crawford, Walt. "Numeracy and common sense: Real-world engineering." *Library Hi Tech* 13:3 (1995): 83-93.

Cross, Patricia. "Mining your automated system for better management: A brief bibliography." *Library Administration & Management* 10:1 (Winter 1996): 26-27.

Florida State Board of Community Colleges. *1998-99 Legislative budget request.* Tallahassee: State Board, 1997.

Florida State Board of Community Colleges. Office of Educational Services and Research. *Library/Learning Resource Centers Program Review, June 1997.* Tallahassee: State Board, 1997.

Hernon, Peter. "Determination of sample size and selection of the sample: Concepts, general sources, and software." *College and Research Libraries* 55:2 (March 1994): 171-179.

Hernon, Peter. "Research and the use of statistics for library decision making." *Library Administration & Management* v.3 (Fall 1989): 176-80.

National Information Standards Organization. *Library Statistics.* Bethesda: NISO, 1997.

Output measures for public libraries: A manual of standardized procedures, by Nancy A. Van House et al. 2nd ed. Chicago: American Library Association, 1987.

Perrault, Anna et al. "An Assessment of the collective resources base of Florida community college library collections: A profile with interpretive analysis." Unpublished study. Tallahassee: College Center for Library Automation and Florida State University School of Library and Information Science, 1996.

Smith, Mark. *Collecting and using public library statistics: A how-to-do-it manual for librarians.* New York: Neal-Schuman, 1996.

Smith, Mark. "Using statistics to increase public library budgets." *The Bottom Line* 9:3 (1996): 4-13.

Decision Support Systems
and Collection Management

Wanda V. Dole

SUMMARY. Libraries have used Decision Support Systems (DSS) to track performance, monitor the results of innovation, identify problems and opportunities, evaluate alternative options, and conduct strategic planning. Until recently, DSS have been underutilized as a collection management tool. This paper explores the potential for and obstacles to computer-based systems for decision support in collection management. *[Article copies available for a fee from The Haworth Document Delivery Service: 1-800-342-9678. E-mail address: <getinfo@haworthpressinc.com> Website: <http://www.haworthpressinc.com>]*

KEYWORDS. DSS (Decision Support Systems), reports, online, strategic planning

DECISION SUPPORT SYSTEMS: DEFINITION AND HISTORY

Decision support systems have been defined as "interactive computer-based systems that help decision makers utilize data and models to solve unstructured problems"[1] or "a computer-based system for identifying, collecting, analyzing and reporting those measures and

---

Wanda V. Dole is Assistant Director of Libraries for Collections & Public Services, State University of New York at Stony Brook, W1508 Melville Library, Stony Brook, NY 11794-3300 USA (e-mail: wdole@ccmail.sunysb.edu).

[Haworth co-indexing entry note]: "Decision Support Systems and Collection Management." Dole, Wanda V. Co-published simultaneously in *The Acquisitions Librarian* (The Haworth Information Press, an imprint of The Haworth Press, Inc.) No. 24, 2000, pp. 47-55; and: *Acquiring Online Management Reports* (ed: William E. Jarvis) The Haworth Information Press, an imprint of The Haworth Press, Inc., 2000, pp. 47-55. Single or multiple copies of this article are available for a fee from The Haworth Document Delivery Service [1-800-342-9678, 9:00 a.m. - 5:00 p.m. (EST). E-mail address: getinfo@haworthpressinc. com].

47

data which are critical in making effective management decisions and plans . . . It is flexible, unstructured, and allows the manager to see new relationships."[2] There is no generally accepted definition of a decision support system, but most descriptions of the systems include the following elements:[3]

1. A database often drawing data from a wide range of sources.
2. Models, generated using the computer and spreadsheet program, to analyze data and to test effects of possible decisions.
3. The end user or decision maker who uses a computer system interactively.
4. Software, capable of managing the database, models, and the interaction between the user and the system. The system must be easy to use, but also powerful and flexible.

Systems such as DSS (decision support systems) that use computer technology to enhance the decision maker's ability to identify, evaluate, and implement decisions are not new. They have been discussed in the literature of management and operations for over 40 years. There is a large body of literature comparing management information systems (MIS) and DSS.[4] The aim of both is to exploit the data-handling and analytical qualities of a computer to provide the type of information that can help managers with decision-making.

MIS were intended to increase the efficiency of managers by producing summary reports based on structured information collected by data processing systems. The reports were generated on a regular basis in a standardized format; exception reports could be produced on demand. Several librarians suggested that MIS, with its ability to cope with routine functions and structured problems, would be useful in library management.[5]

The promise that MIS would help in the efficient running of organizations has not been fulfilled in libraries or in other types of organizations. The literature suggests that the shortcomings of MIS (information overload, canned reports, user-unfriendly systems) combined with advances in technology (low-cost personal computers, increased capability and decreasing cost of telecommunications, increasing availability of public databases and other sources of external data, rapid increases in end-user computing) led to the development of decision support systems.[6]

ADVANTAGES OF DSS TO LIBRARIES

Libraries of all types are increasingly facing the challenges of budgetary constraints, rapidly rising costs, reduced staffing, increased complexity, escalating user demands, rapid technological changes, proliferation of information products and services, and increased demands for accountability from parent institutions or the public. In order to respond to these challenges and to make effective plans and decisions, library managers need timely access to relevant management information and appropriate tools for analysis. Decision support systems can provide the tools to use this information to identify problems, needs and trends and then respond with decisions and programs that allocate resources appropriately.[7]

The collection, storage and transfer of information in libraries is becoming increasingly dependent on technically sophisticated systems. The automated systems support cataloging, circulation, reference, interlibrary loan, and other activities represent a wealth of untapped information for potential use in the planning and management of library resources and service. The technological revolution which brings computers into libraries to automate routine tasks and transactions brings with it a capacity to generate management information.

OBSTACLES TO DECISION SUPPORT SYSTEMS

Although much has been written about the benefits of management information and decision support system, the implementation of such systems in libraries has been slow. The literature suggests the following reasons for lack of implementation:[8]

1. Profit vs. non-Profit. MIS and DSS were developed for business, military and commercial world, not the non-profit sector. Their introduction into the non-profit sector has been more difficult because the model proposed, based on production, marketing and accounting, is not appropriate (for non-profit).
2. Need for support from top management. MIS and DSS need an organizational culture which recognizes the significance of management information as an organizational resource, and in which top level management demonstrates an active commitment to flow of information within the organization.

3. Organizational culture. Unless there is a genuine need for, and an appreciation of, the information produced, then such information may not be utilized. It is possible to produce valid and interesting information on which it is difficult to take action.
4. Fear of out-sourcing or down-sizing. A decision support system could be considered a form of out-sourcing or down-sizing and a threat to department heads/middle managers.
5. Loss of control. DSS breaks down the traditional chain where managers ask subordinates to provide information that is summarized by the subordinate, and about which the manager may subsequently ask questions. The line management chain can be circumvented in the new environment and the concept of "my" information disappears.
6. Quantitative data coming from computer counts can gain validity with some members of staff merely because of the source, but be rejected by others for the same reason.
7. Some staff may develop a dependency upon management information which erodes confidence in their own professional judgment.
8. More and more information may be requested rather than making decisions.
9. Staff expect the same quality of information from unautomated parts of the library system.
10. Fear of statistics/computers. It is necessary to develop a critical approach to quantitative management information amongst librarians who may not be statistically numerate.
11. Not all decisions lend themselves to computer support. Some decisions remain beyond the capacity of computers.
12. External data. Much of the information for a decision support system is generated internally, but externally produced statistics form an important element. While importing such data is not impossible, it is often difficult, because of the different data gathering techniques used and the different methods of presentation to use them as a common input to decision making through their integration into databases and spreadsheets.

SOME RECENT EXAMPLES OF DSS IN LIBRARIES

Although employed in business and industry, DSS have not been widely used in libraries. Recent studies revealed that only 14% of

British libraries[9] and 34% of American research libraries[10] used DSS in library management decisions. Projects using DSS in libraries include an early work by Bommer and Chorba[11] who designed a theoretical decision support system for academic and special libraries.

In 1984, Starratt, Reidelbach and Hartse[12] attempted to initiate a DSS at the University of Nebraska at Omaha. They reported that the attempt, while only partially successful in some respects, yielded results beyond initial expectations. They identified inertia and confusion as the main contributors to the lack of successful implementation.

In 1991 Ottensmann and Gleeson[13] developed a decision support system based on circulation data to assist in public library acquisitions budgeting and other library decision making. The system utilized data generated by a computerized circulation system and was tested by librarians from the Indianapolis-Marion County Public Library. The librarians used the DSS to develop alternative acquisitions budgets, which they reported as being preferred to the existing budgets prepared previously.

In the U.K., there have been major studies of decision support systems at Leicester Polytechnic/De Montfort University (the name of the institution was changed from Leicester Polytechnic to De Montfort in the early 1990s). Leicester Polytechnic Library developed a DSS to help with library resource allocation. The work was carried out as a British Library research project.[14]

Another landmark study at Leicester Polytechnic tested the use of DSS in performance measurement. Bloor[15] examined whether the *Keys to Success* (the manual of performance indicators for public libraries developed by King Research Ltd. at the request of the Office of Arts and Libraries) could be incorporated into a decision support system developed at Leicester. The study tested the relevance and suitability of the *Keys* for use in academic libraries. It confirmed the benefit of following guidelines similar to those suggested by the *Keys* and the value of performance assessment and demonstrated the potential of a DSS to process and analyze the data collected.

Building on the work with the *Keys,* Adams conducted studies at the University (then known as De Montfort) to develop a comprehensive DSS for academic libraries in all areas of library service and management.[16] Another continuation of the work on DSS and performance measures is the Toolbox commissioned by the European Commission and undertaken in 1993 by De Montfort University in partnership with

Essex County Libraries and the Library and Information Statistics Unit (LISU) at Loughborough University.[17] The Toolbox study identified the shortcomings in current performance indicators and proposed a general strategy to make the best use of present computer power.

DEVELOPING A DSS FOR COLLECTION MANAGEMENT

Since 1991, I have been trying to collect data that will help in the rational allocation of the State University of New York at Stony Brook's $3.5 million library materials budget. I have collected data on the cost of library materials, use of serials, ranking of serials, monograph acquisitions, and university priories and tried, with limited success, to build a decision support system.

Between 1991 and 1993, the Stony Brook libraries conducted a one-year journal use study and a journal ranking study to determine the demand for journals by the users of the State University of New York at Stony Brook Libraries. Data collected from these studies were entered into a database that formed the base for a year-long journal review and cancellation project.[18]

In 1993 and in 1996 I used the OCLC/AMIGOS Collection Analysis CD, an interactive pc-based tool, to evaluate the Stony Brook Libraries' monograph acquisitions patterns. In the 1993 study, I used the tool to compare Stony Brook's collecting to university priorities by measuring 1980-1990 acquisitions against those of two sets of peer libraries.[19] In the 1996 study, I used the same tool to compare the collecting patterns of the four members of the State University of New York (SUNY) University Centers consortium.[20] This study provided models for revision of local resource allocation and collection development policies.

Since 1994 I have tried to develop a DSS for the allocation of the library materials budget. The impetus for this DSS was the recommendation by the Stony Brook Libraries 1992 Strategic Plan and the 1993 Collection Analysis Project (CAP) that the Libraries use objective data in distributing the materials budget. In 1994/95, I began allocating the budget by Percentage Based Allocations (PBA), a method by which the percentage of the library materials budget allocated to each discipline is equal to the percentage of the parent institution's instructional and departmental funding (I&DR) received by the corresponding academic department or program.[21] All the factors relating to the university and library users have presumably been applied and weighted by university administrators; therefore, the allocations arrived at are pragmatic and politically defendable in that they reflect the university's strengths and goals as determined by the university administration.

When I modeled the library's acquisitions budget on the university's I&DR budget, I found quantitative support for my suspicion that some departments were receiving too large a share of the budget. I have not, however, been able to make major corrections in the allocations. Stony Brook's materials budget was static from 1991/92 to 1996/97; the Libraries lacked the additional funds needed to correct imbalances in the allocations without taking funds away from some academic departments. Genaway and others recommend that allocations change gradually (no more than plus or minus 10% a year).

Although political realities and lack of financial resources prevented me from fully implementing PBA, I do have the framework for a rational allocation of the materials budget and I made a little progress toward equitable redistribution each year. DSS can be a powerful tool for collection development. It deserves more research, such as replication of the British studies linking DSS and performance measures.

NOTES

1. Gorry, G.A. and Scott-Morton, M.S. "A Framework for Management Information Systems," *Sloan Management Review,* 13 (1971), 55-70.

2. McDonald, Joseph. "Designing a Decision Support System (DSS) for Academic Library Managers Using Preprogrammed Application Software on a Microcomputer," *Library Software Review,* 5/1 (January/February 1986), 9-15.

3. Adams, Roy. "Issues in Decision Support in Libraries," *Information Services and Use,* 11/1-2 (1991), 43-49. Bloor, Ian. *"Keys to Success:* A User's Guide," *Public Library Journal,* 5/6 (November/December 1990), 133-144, and *Performance Indicators and Decision Support Systems for Libraries: A Practical Application of "Keys to Success."* British Library Research Paper 93. Boston Spa: British Library Research and Development Department, 1991.

4. Adams, Roy, Collier, Mel and Meldrum, Marcus. *Decision Support Systems in Academic Libraries.* Library and Information Research Report 83. Cambridge: British Library Board, 1991. Adams, Roy, Bloor, Ian, Collier, Mel, Meldrum, Marcus and Warde, Suzanne. *Decision Support Systems and Performance Assessment in Academic Libraries.* London: Bowker/Saur, 1993.

5. For a review of the literature, see Ferguson, Stuart and Whitelaw, Michael, "Computerised Management Information Systems in Libraries," *Australian Library Journal,* 41/3 (August 1992), 184-198, and Main, Linda, "Decision Support with Decision Making Software," *Library Software Review,* 6/3 (May/June 1987), 128-133.

6. Adams, "Issues," 10-19, and *Decision Support* (1993), 3-4. Ferguson and Whitelaw, "Computerised Management Information Systems," 193-194. Main, Linda. "Computer Simulation and Library Management," *Journal of Library Administration*, 16/4 (1992), 109-130.

7. Bommer, Michael R. W. and Chorba, Ronald W. *Decision Making for Library Management*. White Plains, NY: Knowledge Industry Publications, 1982, p. 23. Cullen, Rowen. "A Model of a Management Information System for Library and Information Service Managers," *International Journal of Information and Library Research*, 2/1 (1990), 23-34.

8. Adams, "Issues," 45-48. Chaudhry, Abdus Sattar. "Automation Systems as Tools of Use Studies and Management Information," *IFLA Journal*, 19/4 (1993), 408. Cullen, "A Model of a Management Information System," Payne, Phillip and Willers, Jean Marie. "Using Management Information in a Polytechnic Library," *Journal of Librarianship*, 21/2 (January 1989), 19-35. Starratt, Joseph; Reidelbach, John; Hartse, Merri. "Developing a Microcomputer-Based Decision Support System: People and Process," *Library Administration and Management*, 4/1 (Winter 1990), 38-41.

9. Richard, Stephen. "Management Information Systems in Academic Libraries," *British Journal of Academic Librarianship*, 4/1 (1989), 49-60.

10. Carrigan, Dennis P. "Data-Guided Collection Development: A Promise Unfulfilled," *College and Research Libraries*, 57/5 (September 1996), 429-437.

11. Bommer and Chorba, *Decision Making for Library Management*. Chorba, Ronald W. and Bommer, Michael R.W. "Developing Academic Library Decision Support Systems," *Journal of the American Society for Information Science*, 34/1 (January 1983), 40-50.

12. Starratt et al. "Developing."

13. Ottensmann, John R. and Gleeson, Michael E. "Implementation and Testing of a Decision Support System for Public Library Materials Acquisitions Budgeting," *Journal of the American Society for Information Science*, 44/2 (March 1993), 83-93. Gleeson, Michael E. and Ottensmann, John R. "Using Data from Computerized Circulation and Cataloging Systems for Management Decisionmaking in Public Libraries," *Journal of the American Society for Information Science*, 44/2 (March 1993), 94-100.

14. Adams, "Issues." Adams et al., *Decision Support* (1991).

15. Bloor, "Keys" and *Performance Indicators*.

16. Adams et al., *Decision Support Systems* (1993).

17. Sumsion, John and Warde, Suzanne. "The Next Generation of Performance Indicators," paper presented at IFLA 1995, Istanbul, Turkey. Paper #018-STAT-2-E.

18. Dole, Wanda V. and Chang, Sherry S. "Survey and Analysis of Demand for Journals at the State University of New York at Stony Brook," *Library Acquisitions: Practice and Theory*, 20/1 (1996), 23-38.

19. Dole, Wanda V. "Myth and Reality: Using the OCLC/AMIGOS Collection Analysis CD to Measure Collections against Peer Collections and against Institutional Priorities," *Library Acquisitions: Practice and Theory*, 18/2 (1994), 179-192.

20. Dole, Wanda V. and Chang, Sherry S. "Consortium Use of the OCLC/AMIGOS Collection Analysis CD: The SUNY Experience," *Library Resources and Technical Services* 41/1 (January 1997), 50-57.

21. Genaway, David C. "PBA: Percentage Based Allocations for Acquisitions," *Library Acquisitions: Practice and Theory*, 10 (1986), 287-292, and "The Q Formula: The Flexible Formula for Library Acquisitions in Relation to the FTE Driven Formula," *Library Acquisitions: Practice and Theory*, 10 (1986), 296-306.

Evaluating Approval Plans
and Other Methods
of Book Selection
Through System Management Reports

Marcia Kingsley

SUMMARY. Basic statistical information that resides in automated circulation and acquisitions systems can be processed to support objective decision-making for developing and refining approval plans. While extracting useful collection management information from most mainframe integrated library systems has been cumbersome, a number of researchers have succeeded in producing exemplary collection management and use studies by using local programming and manual intervention to supplement what their online systems could do. Approval plan managers today can capitalize on the analyses by these librarian-researchers and apply their evaluation techniques specifically to approval plan operations. Librarians also can, or will soon be able to, take advantage of improved data manipulation on newer library management systems with more flexibility and improved report-writing. *[Article copies available for a fee from The Haworth Document Delivery Service: 1-800-342-9678. E-mail address: <getinfo@haworthpressinc.com> Website: <http://www.haworthpressinc.com>]*

KEYWORDS. Reports, online, book selection, approval plans

Collection managers responsible for developing and refining book approval plans can benefit greatly from studying basic statistics re-

Marcia Kingsley is Head of the Serial Resources Department, University Libraries, Western Michigan University, Kalamazoo, MI 49008.

[Haworth co-indexing entry note]: "Evaluating Approval Plans and Other Methods of Book Selection Through System Management Reports." Kingsley, Marcia. Co-published simultaneously in *The Acquisitions Librarian* (The Haworth Information Press, an imprint of The Haworth Press, Inc.) No. 24, 2000, pp. 57-64; and: *Acquiring Online Management Reports* (ed: William E. Jarvis) The Haworth Information Press, an imprint of The Haworth Press, Inc., 2000, pp. 57-64. Single or multiple copies of this article are available for a fee from The Haworth Document Delivery Service [1-800-342-9678, 9:00 a.m. - 5:00 p.m. (EST). E-mail address: getinfo@haworthpressinc.com].

57

lated to categories of new approval books–groupings by subject, call number class, publisher, local bibliographer responsible for the subject area–and their usefulness as measured by in-house and external circulation. In addition, examining approval plan book circulation in comparison to that of firm-orders and gifts can put the approval plan in context and offer some information to suggest desirable changes in collecting patterns.

In many libraries, however, approval plans operate with little local data for librarians to use in objectively assessing the effects of their plans–this despite the sizeable dollar amounts being put into approval collecting year after year. The absence of useful information for measuring approval plan effectiveness probably reflects a similar lack of useable information for all library monographs. However, the likelihood that an approval plan will continue on automatic pilot, adding books in some very low-use areas and perpetually short-changing some heavy-use topics, offers the risk of particularly ineffective spending if management information about approval plan book use is not monitored.

Approval plan vendors have long been able to provide the numbers and average prices of books acquired and rejected by a library, and this information has traditionally been categorized by root call number class, vendor's subject descriptor, or some identifying portion of the profile that generated each hit. This kind of information has been very valuable for collections librarians, especially when the figures can be associated with a particular selector or bibliographer who can actively seek ways to respond to needs not being met by the approval plan.

Yet production of local book-use information such as circulation counts, comparisons of new approval acquisitions to other new books, and figures on proportion of new books to number of holdings already in the collection have had to depend on individual library records and local means of harvesting data. The ability to extract good collection-use information from mainframe integrated library systems has varied with the differing capabilities of the systems, with local management decisions as to whether to buy report-writing software, and with willingness of a library's administration and programming staff to make collection management statistics a priority. Another major factor in acquiring collection management information has been the level of determination and time available for collections and acquisitions librarians to contend with raw data and to create personal computer-based spreadsheets and databases to manipulate them.

A number of librarians have documented their successes at compiling information on monograph use, and these studies provide ideas for replication of their work and, in some cases, building on it to differentiate approval plan book use. Charles Hamaker, for example, has described the kinds of collection management information that can be extracted from even a reluctant system such as NOTIS.[1]

Among his findings, Hamaker found a surprisingly high circulation rate for new books in his library. "Well over 45 percent" of the 24,374 books acquired in a seven-month period had circulated at least once before they were a year old. Hamaker could not calculate more exactly because without additional programming, the system could not omit from the total new book count the branch library books, which did not circulate on the system and therefore artificially deflated the circulation percentage. In another study, Hamaker reported on implications of another sample of new books which showed high initial use and highlighted the need for policies on buying additional copies. He also investigated parts of the collection, identified by LC class, that were receiving a higher proportion of the new books than the percentage of circulation that the areas represented.[2]

Jane Treadwell, examining circulation of certain approval plan books, discovered very high use, including higher use in the undergraduate sciences than in undergraduate humanities.[3] In her essentially manual study, Treadwell garnered extremely pertinent information. Kingsley examined circulation rates of new approval books compared with other kinds of new acquisitions and also broke the information down by basic call number class to see where high and low use existed. A great deal of the information for both these examinations had to be compiled manually.[4]

William Britten and Judith Webster, using statistics from a Geac system, have done extensive analysis of what LC classes and what specific subject headings had unusually high use and deserved special collecting attention.[5] A corollary would be to consider boosting those sections of an approval plan to acquire more in those areas. Other studies where persistence and human labor succeeded in compiling information useful to selectors were described in articles by Robert Baker and by Mike Day and Don Revill. These two studies used information compiled from Dynix systems. While the Recall data retrieval programming under the Pick operating system on Dynix provided some functionality, Baker's value-added project involved incorporating the Dynix information into a database, then use of a word processor to produce discipline-based reports about use and content of the collection which he sent to faculty members.[6]

Day and Revill analyzed by subject area what proportion of new books circulated in their first year of availability and also the number of loans per title. They acknowledged that despite some helpful functions on Dynix, that system and local limitations prevented taking greater steps in their analyses.[7] And Van Gemert, in an interesting management study of lost books, showed that manual checking of online records was necessary to accumulate his data.[8]

The kinds of basic information in all these studies should be at every approval plan manager's fingertips. In the past, the apparently low priority of management reports in the development of most library systems has short-changed collection management. Also, useful collection management information has admittedly presented a real challenge to system functionality and to local programmers because of the disparate locations of data requiring tabulation. For example, mode of acquisition (gift, firm-order, approval plan, standing order) is stored only in acquisitions records in many systems; subject headings are in bibliographic records; call numbers are in bibliographic or auxiliary records such as the copy-holdings records on NOTIS; and circulation information is in patron- and item-records and circulation history files. New systems based on relational databases or object-oriented design should be able to make compilation and reporting of information more straightforward than in the past. As new generation systems are improved and implemented, it should become easier for librarians to obtain their local information similar to what is described in the studies cited above. And information can be expected to be sufficient to answer the kinds of questions suggested below.

WHAT KINDS OF QUESTIONS SHOULD WE BE ABLE TO ANSWER WITH ONLINE SYSTEM INFORMATION ABOUT APPROVAL PLANS?

Raising some questions about what librarians would like to know about approval plans can clarify what it is we should expect from online systems. Below are some of the kinds of questions about approval plans and other methods of selection that can be addressed through system information. These are information needs to consider when evaluating possible new integrated systems and when implementing report functions in newly installed systems. How can approval plans be modified to reflect needs of current users? What can circulation history tell us about book selection "success"? Where in the collection could effective changes be made by changing the approval plan or other collecting methods? What is the average number of circulations for new books that have been available for one year? For two years? For approval books only? What are the averages per call number class? The averages for books purchased on each fund line? How do various classes or funds compare to the norm? And who is using what books?

A base of information would be the average number of circulations for "new" books, defined as all circulating books cataloged and available within a specified time period, as measured one year and/or two years after availability. A useful way to look at the information would be to have average circulations per call number range–again, a matter of definition, depending on how precisely one wants the classification system categorized. A rank ordering of call number ranges as they differ from the norm, or average circulation, would reveal the higher- and lower-use areas. Similarly, having a calculation of percent of new books that have circulated, sorting that information by call number range, and rank-ordering the call number ranges from high circulation rate to low circulation rate would be a valuable survey of the collection.

Call number would be only one area of commonality to look for. Britten and Webster suggested numerous areas of commonality to study in circulation figures, such as language, subject headings, age of books. Another important commonality to examine would be method of purchase, in order to examine patterns of use according to whether books were purchased on an approval plan, through firm-orders, or by other means. Fund-lines used for purchase would be another commonality; especially if funds are associated with individual selectors or are closely related to disciplines, it would be valuable to see which funds' purchases have especially high or low circulation.

Looking at these kinds of data could raise possibilities for adjusting approval plans to increase acquisitions in high-use areas and reduce it in areas of apparent over-collecting. Such information can also provide a reality check to determine the wisdom of local lore. For example, if faculty members in the sciences or other areas consistently indicate that they see no need for any library money to be spent for books in their disciplines, and that all available funds should be used for purchasing journals, it would be useful to see how well books in those disciplines are circulating. Jane Treadwell found that 170 out of 171 books in her sample of new science approval books had circulated at least once within about eighteen months. While 99% of the science books had been checked out, a considerably lower 76% of new humanities approval books had circulated. In this and similar situations, if faculty do not firm-order books because they want only journals, the approval plan and the library bibliographer are important instruments in getting appropriate science books into the library to meet demand.

For the purpose of reality checks, it would be useful to have information by patron category. In academic libraries, one could expect that students rather than faculty are using books in preference to journals, and more undergraduates than graduate students are using books. Those could be false assumptions that would be worth testing. Also, it could be that individuals using many science books, for example those on psychotherapy, drug addiction, and personality disorders, are faculty and students in the social sciences and education. Collection managers should consequently keep in mind, therefore, that approval plan and firm-order allocations being spent in such subjects are supporting multi-disciplinary use.

These are just a few of the ways in which management statistics for approval plan books can assist in developing effective collections by responding to user needs in order to predict what books will actually be used. Similarly, shifting spending away from low-use areas could reduce funds spent on books that will never or rarely be used.

How can the approval plan enhance the efficiency of getting quality new books into the library? What is the "normal" ratio of new books purchased by approval plan versus bibliographic notification form versus firm-order, gift, and standing order? What areas of the circulating collection vary substantially or significantly from the norm?

If the average purchase method for all new books acquired is 45% approval plan, 45% firm-order, and 10% other, those averages can be used as the norms. Examining the variations from the norms where percentages differ greatly can provide further understanding of collecting patterns. Again the next step is to look for commonalities. Seeing the mode-of-acquisitions analyzed by call number, by fund, by bibliographer, or by publisher would highlight areas of substantial variations from the overall ratio of approval plan, firm-order, and other receipts. Of course, some areas would show understandable differences; in specialized disciplines, where a library tries to maintain a comprehensive collection, higher than average firm-ordering would make sense in order to bring in specialized books that may not be covered by an approval plan vendor. But aside from topics where major variations seem appropriate, figures can provide management a view of how collecting can become more efficient. Areas of very high firm-ordering that could be shifted to approval coverage or notification slip coverage would reduce firm orders, selectors' time, paperwork, and possibly price.

Another commonality whose recognition could lead to more efficient collecting is publisher. Obtaining a frequency count by publisher for new books, then categorizing that information by method of acquisition, could reveal publishers for whom the library is doing a great deal of firm-ordering. Those presses could be considered for a special purchasing plan, blanket order, or very broad profile. Unfortunately, even if one can obtain the publisher-purchase information readily from a local automated system, the online catalog won't be able to provide a snapshot of how many books the publishers published in a year in order to see what proportion of books the library is acquiring. However, searching an electronic version of *Books in Print* to find publishing output figures for selected publishers would be easy. With a select list of publishers from whom the library is acquiring a high proportion of titles, it would be necessary to appraise the publishers for quality, perhaps with reference to a recent article by Paul Metz and John Stemmer, and place certain publishers on a blanket order.[9]

The above are the kinds of management information that can help refine approval plans and make the acquisitions and collection development operations more efficient by eliminating unnecessary individual selection and ordering.

CONCLUSION

With new tools available, approval plan managers will be able to capitalize on system statistics to develop empirical bases for evaluating success of approval plan collecting compared with other methods of book selection. Even such basic functions as frequency counts, averages, sorting by selected fields, and rank ordering have enormous potential. Without necessarily including any statistical functions such as tests of significance, reports showing patterns of information will be a substantial improvement in management information support for most approval plans. The information potentially can be used not only by approval plan managers but can be extracted for individual bibliographers and selectors. For conscientious book selectors, feedback on patron use of the books acquired through "their" portions of the approval plan, current firm-order selections, and vendor notification forms or slips would be welcome and enlightening.

REFERENCES

1. Charles A. Hamaker, "Management Data for Selection Decisions in Building Library Collections," *Journal of Library Administration*, 17 (2) (1992), 71-97.

2. Charles A. Hamaker, "Some Measures of Cost Effectiveness in Library Collections," *Journal of Library Administration*, 16 (3) (1992), 57-69.

3. Jane Treadwell, "Circulation Patterns of Recent Imprints," in *First Century: Proceedings of the Fifth International Conference of the Association of College and Research Libraries*. Chicago: ACRL, 1989, 230-234.

4. Marcia S. Kingsley, "Circulation Statistics for Measuring Approval Plan Effectiveness," *Against the Grain*, 8 (4) (September, 1996) 1, 16-17.

5. William A. Britten and Judith D. Webster, "Class Relationships: Circulation Data, Collection Development Priorities, and Funding for the Future," *The Bottom Line*, 4 (1) (1990), 8-11. William A. Britten and Judith D. Webster, "Comparing Characteristics of Highly Circulated Titles for Demand-Driven Collection Development," *College and Research Libraries*, 53 (3) (May, 1992), 239-248.

6. Robert A. Baker, "Using a Turnkey Automated System to Support Collection Assessment," *College and Research Libraries*, 51 (4) (July, 1990), 360-366.

7. Mike Day and Don Revill, "Towards the Active Collection: The Uses of Circulation Analyses in Collection Evaluation," *Journal of Librarianship and Information Science*, 27 (3), (September, 1995), 149, 157.

8. Edward V. Van Gemert, "Where Have All the Lost Books Gone?" *C & R L News*, 57 (9) (October, 1996), 581-583.

9. Paul Metz and John Stemmer, "A Reputational Study of Academic Publishers," *College and Research Libraries*, 57 (3) (May, 1996), 234-47.

Integrating Vendor Supplied Management Reports for Serials Evaluation: The Medical College of Wisconsin Experience

Alfred Kraemer
Michael Markwith

SUMMARY. Large price increases as well as the need to subscribe to new journals in key research areas underscore the need for improved analysis of journal price and use information. This article outlines a process used at a medical research library in which local use data and vendor information are integrated to produce management reports. The underlying data must provide the flexibility to produce and evaluate a variety of options. A more standardized approach would benefit libraries as well as vendors. *[Article copies available for a fee from The Haworth Document Delivery Service: 1-800-342-9678. E-mail address: <getinfo@haworthpressinc.com> Website: <http://www.haworthpressinc.com>]*

KEYWORDS. Serials management, serials acquisition, serial publications-cost studies, journal use studies, serials evaluation, online reports

Alfred Kraemer, MLIS, University of Wisconsin-Milwaukee, is Head of Technical Services, Medical College of Wisconsin Libraries, 8701 Watertown Plank Road, Milwaukee, WI 53226 (e-mail: akraemer@post.its.mcw.edu).

Michael Markwith is Chief Executive Officer, Swets & Zeitlinger, Inc., 440 Creamery Way, Suite A, Exton, PA 19341 (e-mail: mmarkwith@swetsinc.com).

[Haworth co-indexing entry note]: "Integrating Vendor Supplied Management Reports for Serials Evaluation: The Medical College of Wisconsin Experience." Kraemer, Alfred, and Michael Markwith. Co-published simultaneously in *The Acquisitions Librarian* (The Haworth Information Press, an imprint of The Haworth Press, Inc.) No. 24, 2000, pp. 65-73: *Acquiring Online Management Reports* (ed: William E. Jarvis) The Haworth Information Press, an imprint of The Haworth Press, Inc., 2000, pp. 65-73. Single or multiple copies of this article are available for a fee from The Haworth Document Delivery Service [1-800-342-9678, 9:00 a.m. - 5:00 p.m. (EST). E-mail address: getinfo@haworthpressinc.com].

Every time the annual journal price increases exceed the amount bud-
geted for journal subscriptions, libraries are put under increased pressure
to justify their subscription decisions. Nowhere else is the journal price
pressure more severe than in research libraries with a large number of
STM journals. There is no shortage of articles reporting on the devastat-
ing effects of double-digit subscription price increases on library budgets
in research libraries. Chrzastowski and Schmidt evaluated the cumulative
impact on the collections of ten large academic research libraries and
showed large reductions in current serial holdings.[1]

There is also dominant and prevailing wisdom that serials vendors
work together with libraries seeking win/win solutions that utilize the
benefits of the vendor's business acumen with the library's need to
maximize its limited financial resources.

Responsibility of serials vendors includes more than just insuring
the timely renewal and delivery of serials ordered by customers. A
primary example is providing all financial data pertaining to a customer's orders as well as management reports that both explain and fore-
cast budget expenditures. After all, serials consume a minimum of
60% of most research library budgets. In many instances the share of
serials expenditures is closer to 75-80%.

Swets and the Medical College of Wisconsin have participated in a
business relationship since 1988. As the primary serials vendor, Swets
is responsible for providing accurate and timely financial data for
price information, budget decisions and collection development decisions to retain or cancel a title. Medical College of Wisconsin's reporting needs, just like all libraries', require more information and data
than Swets, or any serials vendor, can provide. This article presents the
process and practical application of MCW's management report needs
and stresses the need for better data and information in the retrospective and prospective evaluation of journal collections.[2]

CHANGES IN JOURNAL EVALUATION METHODS

In response to the subscription inflation price crisis, many academic
research libraries have put greater emphasis on gathering and analyzing local data on the utilization of the journal collection with the goal
of determining the relationship between usage and price for each
subscription title. Nearly all of the recent journal utilization studies
differ from older, manual methods in several key aspects:

- the design takes the capabilities of integrated library systems into account.
- price and use data must be combined by a valid mechanism to provide cost/benefit information.
- the use data is not limited to a small portion of the journal collection but focuses instead on the entire journal collection. This is significant since it allows the calculation of relative costs and benefits.
- the availability of comprehensive utilization data makes it suitable for many decision-making purposes: budgeting, projecting local usage trends, and other planning tasks.
- database programs run on more powerful computers are able to merge and help analyze data from multiple sources.

The methodologies devised for such comprehensive data gathering and analysis are still in an early stage of development. However, in conjunction with vendors (subscription agencies, bibliographic utilities, etc.), libraries can produce management reports which put decision-making on a much firmer footing.

The first method outlined in this article has been used over the past four years at the Medical College of Wisconsin Libraries. Reshelving data was recorded in the local INNOPAC integrated library system and invoicing information from the serials vendor, SWETS, is linked to journal order records in the INNOPAC system. Although the method described below was initially devised to help select subscriptions to be canceled, it became evident that this task had to be tied in with a broader evaluation of the serials collection.

Objectives

The main rationale for serials management reports is the ability to support decision-making with reliable and detailed empirical data. However, after initial discussions which included library staff, administration, and faculty representatives, two key priorities for data collection emerged:

1. local usage data would be at the core of the annual evaluation of active subscriptions. Several other criteria, e.g., the price per published page, etc., were deliberately excluded as they are not a reliable indicator of a journal's value.

2. local usage for a title should be compared annually to the cost of retaining the subscription. This is often referred to as the "Cost per use."

General indicators of journal relevance, e.g., ISI Journal Citation Rankings, which were recommended in many earlier models for journal cancellation decisions, were to be used as a secondary criterion, e.g., as a tie-breaker.[3]

After an examination of the INNOPAC use data fields and their functioning, it was decided that use data would be gathered by serial title. Although this method favors serials with large holdings, it was felt it could accomplish the main initial goal of identifying serials with very low usage. The objection that some uses would be missed recording reshelving data was not seen as a significant drawback since there was no indication that unrecorded reshelving would affect one journal more than another. This point was well defined at NASIG workshop on the design of journal use studies where presenters distinguished between absolute and relative use data.[4]

Similarly, the cost-per-use was more accurately defined as a way to compare the annual local usage for a journal title with the cost of continuing the subscription and the costs of alternatives to a subscription, e.g., document delivery.

As expected, the task of locating journals which could be cancelled with a minimal impact on library patrons becomes increasingly difficult after several rounds of cancellations and calls for more refined methods of cost/benefit analysis.

At the Medical College of Wisconsin, management reports on journal usage and cost/benefit ratios were never intended to replace faculty input, on the contrary, the reports have become a vital part of the library's interaction with faculty committees as well as individual departments.

In summary, the initial goal of minimizing the impact of inevitable subscription cancellations is being replaced by the broader goal of maximizing the benefit of the library's journal collection for its patrons in the light of changing journal needs, continuing price increases, and the availability of alternatives to subscriptions.

DATA SOURCES FOR JOURNAL MANAGEMENT REPORTS

Three different data sources form the basis of most management reports:

1. The "Circulation Statistics by Title" table from the local IN-NOPAC catalog. This function compiles different usage fields (checkout, internal use, and an editable use field used for retaining usage data after binding).
2. Price information from the subscription agency with price, subscription period, and order record number which corresponds with the order record in the library's system. This data is supplied in a delimited format and can be easily loaded into the INNOPAC system as well as the database for creating management reports.
3. A separate table with information taken from the bibliographic record with fields for title, publisher, succeeding/preceding title(s), and some fixed fields.

These tables are loaded into a Microsoft ACCESS database. The above data tables share certain fields (Order record number, ISSNs/OCLC number) which are used for merging. Relational database software packages such as ACCESS make complex merging operations a quick and accurate task, if caution is observed in defining the merging parameters.

DATA INPUTTING AND COLLECTION METHOD

Reshelving data is recorded by scanning the barcode which is found on every journal item, bound or unbound. The binding of unbound volumes is governed by procedures which ensure the retention of reshelving information.

INTEGRATING VENDOR DATA

Vendor-supplied invoice data–price, subscription period, invoice number, and a reference number shared with the library's acquisition module–must meet these requirements to be useful in usage/price calculations:

- it must be in an importable format, e.g., a delimited file.
- the shared reference number with the library's database has to be maintained, e.g., if a title change occurs, the reference number moves on to the new title.
- invoice dates must be included in separate fields so that the annual cost for subscription as well as series titles can be calculated accurately in the database.

EVALUATING THE IMPACT OF CANCELLATIONS

An expected outcome of cancellations is an increase of interlibrary loan figures for the dropped subscriptions. Four years after the first round of cancellations none of the titles cancelled has appeared on the report of titles requested via interlibrary loan more than five times in one year. This will undoubtedly change if the cut-off point for low-usage has to be raised to reconcile the total cost of journal subscriptions with the journal budget.

So far the cancellations have had no impact on the total usage for our active journal titles, despite the significant decrease of journal subscriptions. Although many factors may have influenced this statistic, it also can be seen as an indicator of success in canceling journals with a least impact on the usage total.

A very positive effect has been the support the library has received from faculty for the method employed for journal cancellations. The review of past cancellations has also underscored the need for a more detailed breakdown of usage data. For future cancellation projects it will be imperative to take a look at the usage not only by title, but also by specific years for each journal title. A proposed, and partially implemented, method for such use data collection is described below.

REVIEW AND REDESIGN
OF THE DATA COLLECTION PROCESS

The most important deficiency of usage data collection by title is the effect of varying size of holdings for each title on the total usage figure. While this may be acceptable when cancellations are based on very low use figures, this deficiency becomes unacceptable if previous cancellations have exhausted the pool of journal titles with overall low use totals.

The level of detail in usage reports has a direct impact on the usefulness of price comparisons among journal subscriptions as well as on the accuracy of comparisons between subscription and document delivery costs. If reliable price-per use data cannot be limited to recent holdings, projections about the impact of journal subscriptions will have a large error margin.

The redesign of the use data collection centered on the fact that use data in INNOPAC–and in most other systems–accumulate in the item record. Since the item record also contains a formatted volume information field, item information can be extracted and compiled on a publication year basis, i.e., a more detailed use data analysis is possible (Figure 1).

After estimating the effect of this approach on database size and assessing the information needs for evaluating active subscriptions, the decision was made to limit the year-by-year breakdown to the last five years.

The implications for the management of the data are considerable: at the Medical College of Wisconsin the number of records in the database used to be about 1,800, in agreement with the number of active journal titles. After including all item records for active journals from the last five years, the database size jumped to more than 40,000 records (see Figure 2). However, managing even large datasets is not beyond the scope of high-end personal computers.

Such detailed usage data will provide a much clearer picture of utilization of recent years of a journal's holdings. In addition, multiple subscriptions can be analyzed separately by location since a location field is part of the item record in the library's catalog.

FIGURE 1. Example of Use Data Collection by Year

1997 USAGE DATA		
Title: *International Journal of X*		
	Usage (1997)	Previous Year (1996)
Total usage:	**897**	**865**
Usage for 1997 vols:	98	–
Usage for 1996 vols:	124	102
Usage for 1995 vols:	112	128

BEYOND CANCELLATIONS:
MATCHING JOURNAL DEMAND AND BUDGET

Continuing cancellation cycles is an undertaking with diminishing returns: once low-usage journals have been cut, future cancellations will include journals with higher usage levels. Soon a point is reached where the costs, e.g., document delivery to supply demand, will outweigh the benefits of cancellation.

Summary reports reflecting the impact of various cancellation scenarios underscore the need for appropriate funding (see Figure 3).

Many other reports can readily be produced when needed. Although every library has unique needs for management reports, the discussion of journal evaluation methods and resulting management reports at conferences and in journal articles demonstrates–in our opinion–that the development of standards–or "best practices"–for serial evaluation procedures is desirable and possible. Black presents a model for serials collection analysis with different emphasis but similar report categories.[5]

CONCLUSIONS

There are many factors that indicate an increasing demand for management reports derived from use and price information: the likely

FIGURE 2. Sample of a Table with Raw Item Record Data

ID	BIB#	Item#	LOCATION	Checkout	IntlU	Vol
9889	b10641865	il2345192	twper	0	28	v. 13 no.4 (1994: Oct.)
9887	b10678864	il2345209	twper	3	15	v. 10 no.4 (1994: Oct.)
9888	b10648902	il234560x	muper	7	22	v. 74 no.5 (1994: Oct.)
9889	b10645317	il2345611	muper	12	34	v. 37 (1992)+ suppl.

FIGURE 3. Summary Report: High Cost-Per-Use Journals

Groups	Price Tot/Group	Cum. Price Total	Tot # of Uses in Group
Cost per Use $75-100 + Uses in 1996 > 20 (1 Title)	9,037.44	$9,037.44	183
Cost per Use $50-75 + Uses in 1996 > 20 (27 Titles)	$31,210.53	$40,247.97	631
Cost per Use $25-50 + Uses in 1996 > 20 (52 Titles)	$82,868.64	$123,116.61	2728

continuation of journal price increases that outpace the rate of inflation, changes in research focus and corresponding needs for subscription changes, library space utilization, and new technologies for the delivery of information. Librarians will very likely be expected to use advanced information and data management tools. Even a very cursory look at reports on "data warehousing," "data mining" provides a glimpse into data management tools that could be adapted to produce management reports for library settings.

As helpful as these tools may be for producing detailed management reports, the design, compilation, and interpretation of such reports has to be guided by a clear understanding of the role of journal collections for a library's constituency. Management reports with comprehensive, accurate, and relevant utilization data are critical in reaching broadly-supported decisions about serials subscriptions. While current models of management reports for library settings–including the one outlined in this article–vary considerably and may have significant limitations, current pressures to improve accountability of library fund allocation are likely to lead to better, more standardized, library management reports.

NOTES

1. Chrzastowski, Tina E. and Karen A. Schmidt, "The Serials Cancellation Crisis: National Trends in Academic Library Serials Collections," *Library Acquisitions: Practice & Theory* 21, no. 4 (1997): 431-443.

2. Richards, Daniel T. and Antonija Prelec, "Serials Cancellation Projects: Necessary Evil or Collection Assessment Opportunity?," *The Serials Librarian* 24, no. 3-4 (1992): 31-45.

3. Broadus, Robert, "A Proposed Method for Eliminating Titles from Periodical Subscription Lists," *College & Research Libraries* 46 (1985): 30-35.

4. Edelmann, Marla, "Designing Effective Journal Use Studies," *The Serials Librarian* 24, no.3/4 (1994): 189-192.

5. Black, Steve, "Journal Collection Analysis at a Liberal Arts College," *Library Resources and Technical Services* 41, no. 4 (1997): 283-294.

Instant Access
to Fund Accounting Information:
Advice for Selectors
and Acquisitions Librarians

Teri L. Oparanozie

SUMMARY. One of the needs of selectors has been to obtain fund accounting information on demand. Most integrated library systems with acquisitions modules make it possible for selectors to view fund information online at their convenience. Fluctuations that occur in fund balances as orders are placed, invoiced, or canceled are more noticable when funds are frequently reviewed online. To help selectors interpret these fluctuations, acquisitions departments need to better define the timeframes or schedules for activities that cause these changes. At a medium-size academic library, arrangements were made for selectors to view fund records online in the DRA (Data Research Associates) acquisitions module. The steps followed are described along with other information to help selectors interpret fund transactions. Short cuts for running and printing the DRA Fund Nesting Report are also included. *[Article copies available for a fee from The Haworth Document Delivery Service: 1-800-342-9678. E-mail address: <getinfo@haworthpressinc.com> Website: <http://www.haworthpressinc.com>]*

KEYWORDS. BCL3, DRA, fund nesting, online reports

Teri L. Oparanozie is Head of Acquisitions, Newton Gresham Library, Sam Houston State University, 1804 Avenue H, Huntsville, TX 77341 (email: LIB_TLO@SHSU.EDU).

[Haworth co-indexing entry note]: "Instant Access to Fund Accounting Information: Advice for Selectors and Acquisitions Librarians." Oparanozie, Teri L. Co-published simultaneously in *The Acquisitions Librarian* (The Haworth Information Press, an imprint of The Haworth Press, Inc.) No. 24, 2000, pp. 75-88; and: *Acquiring Online Management Reports* (ed: William E. Jarvis) The Haworth Information Press, an imprint of The Haworth Press, Inc., 2000, pp. 75-88. Single or multiple copies of this article are available for a fee from The Haworth Document Delivery Service [1-800-342-9678, 9:00 a.m. - 5:00 p.m. (EST). E-mail address: getinfo@haworthpressinc.com].

INTRODUCTION

At the beginning of the movie *Forrest Gump*, the flight of a feather is followed as it falls from the sky. Gravity is pulling it towards the earth but it does not fall in a straight line. It twists and turns, rises and falls, and flutters this way and that as it glides past rooftops and treetops. At one point as it nears the earth, the feather almost alights on a man's shoulder but resumes its fall as he steps forward out of its path. Then it nearly touches down in the middle of a busy street when the wind from a passing car lifts it up towards Forrest Gump who is sitting on a bench waiting for his bus to arrive. As it settles at his feet, Forrest picks up the feather, admires it for a few moments, then opens his briefcase and places it inside the pages of the book *Curious George*. The flight of the feather is an apt metaphor for the fluctuations that occur in monographic fund balances during the course of a fiscal year. The working balance fluctuates up and down as various transactions occur but eventually it falls to zero if the selector submits enough orders to encumber or expend all of the allocation.

One of the functions of acquisitions departments is to provide services to librarians who have collection development responsibilities.[1] These services include processing orders, supplying fund accounting information, and keeping selectors informed about acquisitions procedures which impact the selection process. Most integrated library systems with acquisitions modules make it easy for acquisitions librarians to provide printed fund reports to selectors. In fact, some systems allow selectors to view fund records from their own computers at their convenience. Selectors who frequently review fund records online often become aware of, and want to know what is causing, the fluctuations in their funds. They may ask acquisitions librarians to provide time-frames and schedules for acquisition routines which affect their funds.

The particular routines that are most carefully scrutinized depend in part on the automated system the library is using, as well as the related policies and procedures of the acquisitions department. As Karen Schmidt said about variations in pre-order searching, "It would appear that practically every library has its own definition of which of these and other procedures embrace pre-order searching, based in part on the automated systems available to each library and the organizational arrangements which each has made."[2] Once the key transactions affecting fund accounting have been identified, acquisitions librarians may want to perform time analyses of the related routines to define them more precisely and make them better known to selectors so that interpretation of online fund information will be improved.

Sam Houston State University (SHSU) has a student enrollment of approximately 11,000. There are four colleges: Arts and Sciences, Business Administration, Criminal Justice, and Education and Applied Sciences. Bachelor's, master's, and two doctoral degrees are offered. The university has a centralized library, the Newton Gresham Library (NGL), with fourteen librarians and twenty-six para-professionals. The library collection contains more than 1.3 million books, bound periodicals, and government documents. The library uses the DRA (Data Research Associates) integrated library system for acquisitions, cataloging, circulation, reserves, serials check-in, and public catalog functions. DRA Classic version 2.5 is run with the VMS version 6.2 operating system.

NGL does not have an approval plan for acquiring monographic materials. Firm orders are selected by the fourteen librarians who each have authority over their particular subject funds. The librarians (i.e., selectors) discuss needs for library materials with faculty liaisons in the academic departments that correspond to their subject funds. Selectors are responsible for monitoring their funds to ensure that the orders submitted are within the amounts allocated by the Head of Collection Development.

To keep selectors abreast of fund balances, the acquisitions librarian ran, printed, and distributed the DRA Fund Nesting Report once a month. Some selectors expressed an interest in receiving the report on a weekly basis while others preferred to receive it quarterly. In order to give selectors control over accessing fund information at times most convenient to them, adjustments were made to their acquisitions security records. Instructions were provided for how to access the fund records from their own computer accounts. A brief description of the fund record fields was also given to them.

The arrangements for allowing selectors to view DRA monographic fund records online from their own computer accounts, as well as the short cuts for running and printing the DRA Fund Nesting Report, are described. Basic book-purchasing practices in academic libraries and fund accounting fundamentals are discussed to help selectors better understand the online fund records and fund reports. In anticipation of questions that often arise as selectors become more aware of fluctuations in their funds, the key transactions affecting fund accounting in the DRA acquisitions system and corresponding acquisitions routines used at the Newton Gresham Library are identified.

BOOK PURCHASING IN ACADEMIC LIBRARIES

Selectors are interested in fund accounting because it helps them track the amount of money they have spent and/or still have available for book orders. There are many variables in the book purchasing process that make it difficult for selectors to know precisely how much money is available for new orders at any given point in time. Titles that are currently on order may never be received, the price may vary from what is expected, or books may be received and then be returned. Replacement copies for returned books may or may not be obtained. The following discussion of the book-purchasing process explains some of the reasons for these uncertainties.

Purchasing books in academic libraries usually includes several basic steps.

- Selectors submit book orders.
- Pre-order searching is done to verify titles and ensure that items are not owned or on order.
- Purchase orders are created and sent to suppliers.
- Suppliers receive purchase orders and send the books with invoices.
- The acquisitions department receives the books and makes arrangements to pay the invoices.

Of course, obtaining books for an academic library is much more complex than just described. It is easy to assume that a book listed in a publisher's catalog or reviewed in a journal will be available and that the price will be the amount quoted there. However, there is often only a short period of time during which the book can actually be obtained. The availability of a book may be thought of as a window opening and closing. The window may open and close several times for each title. Books are often advertised before they are published to determine the demand for the title. During this prepublication period the book is not really available so the window is closed. However, an order can be placed so that when the title is published, a copy will be sent. Unfortunately, the publication of some titles is delayed months, years, or indefinitely. To prevent money being tied up in an order indefinitely, libraries generally specify an automatic cancellation period so that the order is canceled if it is not received within that time. The period is usually three to twelve months. When a book is published the window of availability is open for a while until all of the copies have been sold. The title is then listed as out of stock and the window is closed again. However, a back-order may be placed if it is expected that more copies will be printed and a copy will be sent when available. Eventually, the publisher may decide that no more copies will be printed, and the book is listed as out of print. All back-orders are canceled and the window of availability is closed again.

The availability of books is also affected by the choice of vendor. Vendors vary greatly in their abilities to obtain books. Some vendors have large warehouses of trade or popular titles which they can supply quickly. Other vendors have little inventory but have expertise in contacting publishers and handling hard-to-obtain items. If a book order is not filled by one vendor, it may be canceled and reordered with another supplier whose expertise or luck in finding the window of availability open results in obtaining the book.

When ordering a book, it is difficult for the selector to know the exact amount that will be spent on the book even if a list price is given in a publisher's catalog. Academic libraries usually order from book vendors, although some orders are sent directly to publishers. The library often receives discounts from vendors based on the discounts the vendors receive from the publishers. Depending on the type of book, discounts vary widely from nearly 50% for some trade titles to no discount at all. A service fee may be charged for others. Vendors also vary discounts depending on the amount of business they receive from a library. The library may order the same title from one vendor at a 5% discount but at a 15% discount from another vendor. Another factor affecting price is the amount of time that has elapsed from when the book was published until it is ordered. When a book goes into a second or subsequent printing, it may be more expensive than the first printing. Or, a paperback version may be published at substantially less cost than the hardback.

When the book is received, if all is well, it will be kept. However, there are numerous reasons why books may be returned: damaged during shipping, wrong edition, wrong binding, or wrong book sent. In some cases the library finds that the book was ordered by mistake or that it is a duplicate copy. If a book is returned to the vendor, the correct copy may be requested on the original order or a new order may be placed. In either case, the replacement copy may or may not be received due to the same factors listed above.

To interpret online fund records or printed fund reports, selectors must understand the fundamentals of fund accounting for the book-purchasing process. In the next section, some basics of fund accounting will be discussed along with a description of DRA fund records and Fund Nesting Reports as used in the Newton Gresham Library.

FUND ACCOUNTING FUNDAMENTALS

Monographic funds in academic libraries usually correspond to academic departments such as art, sociology, and English. At NGL, there are about fifty funds. Money is allocated to the funds based on factors such as department size and levels of academic programs (i.e., undergraduate, masters, doctoral). At NGL for the past few years, an initial allocation was given to each fund at the beginning of the fiscal year, and adjustments were made during the year as money became available for the monographic budget. At the end of the fiscal year, the fund is closed. Before closing it, any remaining portion of the allocation for books ordered but not received that fiscal year is rolled into the next fiscal year's fund. This is called the "carried allocation" as opposed to the "current allocation." The DRA online fund records have editable fields for the "current allocation" and "carried allocation." The system adds these two fields together and displays a "total allocation" field which cannot be edited.

As discussed above, the exact amount that will be spent on a book is often not known at the time it is ordered. However, an estimate of the cost based on the list price and the estimated discount should be encumbered on the fund. When books are ordered, the net cost of each book is added to the encumbrance field of the appropriate fund and subtracted from its working balance. This helps the selector to know how much money is expected to be spent even though the estimate could be off by several hundred dollars (e.g., thirteen books ordered at an estimated discount of 18% were invoiced with a 41.6% discount and thereby cost $195 less than expected). In the DRA fund records, there are "carried encumbrance," "current encumbrance," and "total encumbrance" fields similar to the allocation fields. Encumbrances are carried from one fiscal year to another for books that are still on order.

When books are received, the estimated costs are disencumbered and the actual costs are expended. For example, when an art book that was encumbered for $100 is invoiced for $150, the $100 is subtracted from the current encumbrance for the art fund and is added back into its working balance. The $150 is added to the expenditures for the art fund and is subtracted from its working balance. In the DRA fund records, there is only one field for "expenditures" representing the amount actually spent for titles received during the fiscal year.

When book orders are canceled for any reason (e.g., out of print, not received within automatic cancellation period, duplicate copy), the estimated costs are disencumbered. The money is added back into the working balances of the affected funds to be used for new orders. Or, the canceled titles are ordered again from another vendor and the money is re-encumbered for them.

The "cash balance" and "working balance" fields are calculated based on the other fields. They are not editable in the DRA fund record. The cash balance is the total allocation minus the expenditures. It reflects the amount of the allocation that is remaining after subtracting money spent on orders that have actually been received. The working balance is the total allocation minus the expenditures minus the total encumbrances. This is the amount of money available for new orders based on the estimated cost of the titles currently on order and the amount spent on titles received. The working balance constantly fluctuates up and down as titles are ordered, invoiced, and canceled. It eventually decreases to zero if the selector submits enough orders to encumber and/or spend all of the money during the fiscal year.

AUTHORIZING SELECTORS
TO VIEW FUND RECORDS ONLINE

The fields that can be viewed online in the DRA fund records include: carried allocation, current allocation, total allocation, carried encumbrance, current encumbrance, total encumbrance, total expended, cash balance, and working balance. The records also display total encumbrance, total expended, cash balance, and working balance as percentages of the total allocation.

Selectors can easily be given the authority to view these fund records online. The DRA system has security records for the various components of the system such as cataloging, circulation, and acquisitions. The systems librarian has the authority to access the security records and set the level of privileges for each person who has an account. In the acquisitions profile, if column G for "Funds" is set to "yes" for "inquire" level, this will allow the selectors to view funds and fund transactions. They will also be able to view bibliographic records associated with the fund transactions.

Selectors can be given a simple set of instructions for accessing the fund records similar to the following. (System prompt refers to the VMS system prompt.)

1. At the system prompt, type: **run drapgm:acquisitions,** and press "return."
2. At the Acquisitions Menu, type **f** for "Fund Information," and press "return."
3. At the Fund Processing menu, type **f** for "Find a fund," and press "return."
4. At Enter Fund ID: (type the fund ID used by your library. For example, M-ASB-SOC is the sociology fund ID at NGL).
5. At Beginning of Date Range: (enter the beginning date of the fund or press "return" for the default).
6. At End of Date Range: (enter the end date of the fund which is usually the end of the fiscal year or press "return" for the default).
7. The fund record should appear. The amounts displayed in the fields will reflect the transactions which have occurred to that point in time.

FUND NESTING REPORT SHORTCUTS

The DRA Fund Nesting Report pulls the following fields from the online fund record for display in the printed report: total allocation, total encumbered, total expended, cash balance, and working balance. The percentage of the total allocation is also given for each field. At the bottom of the report the funds are totaled for each field.

The Fund Nesting Report can be run in about five minutes using the following shortcuts. This is in contrast to waiting for the report to run overnight and print at the system printer which may be in another building as it is at SHSU. The acquisitions librarian or person running the report needs to have access to the VMS system prompt. The person's acquisitions security profile must have column H for "Reports" set to yes for "inquire" level. This allows reports to be run which do not update records. The Fund Nesting Report does not update records; it merely reports data from the online fund records.

Much time is saved by setting up abbreviations for commands in the login.com file. Abbreviations are set up by typing the letters selected for the abbreviation followed by a colon, two equal signs, and the command. At NGL the login.com file is edited by typing **eve login.com** at the system prompt. Four abbreviations can be set up by typing the following at the system prompt in the login.com file.

> **sysq :==sho que sys$batch** [This will display the job queue which runs reports overnight.]

> **setd :==set entry/reque=dra$batch** [This will re-queue the job.]

> **draq :==sho que dra$batch/all** [This will display the DRA queue which runs jobs immediately instead of waiting overnight.]

> **fnr :==list acq_fund_nesting_report.lst** [This is the command for printing the report once it has been run.]

After entering these commands, press the F10 or Control-Z keys to exit the login.com file. To view the login.com file without editing it, at the system prompt enter **type login.com.** Activate the commands by typing **@login** at the system prompt or by logging off and back on.

The Fund Nesting Report is accessed by selecting "Reports and Notices" from the "Acquisitions" menu. Under the category "FUNDS" are two reports. Select the line number for the "Nesting" report. The criteria for the report must be specified. At NGL the monographic funds for the current fiscal year are selected. This report format is saved so that the next time the report is run the "GetLast" command is used to bring up the last set of criteria that was saved. Once the criteria and sort options have been set up, select "DoReport" instead of "PrintReport." A message will appear on the screen that says, "Report has been submitted. Press a key." When any key is pressed, the menu bar at the bottom of the screen will appear as "Criteria, Sort, GetLast, DoReport, PrintReport." Press "return" to bring up the save bar (i.e., "Save, Quit, or Continue?") with "Save" as the default. Press "return." The "Reports and Statistics" menu reappears. Press "return" or F10 or Control-Z. At the "Which number?" prompt, press "return." The "Acquisitions" menu reappears. Press "return" or F10 to exit to the system prompt.

To re-queue the DRA command file so that the Fund Nesting Report will run immediately and print to port, use the following abbreviated commands set up previously in the login.com file.

- At the system prompt, type **sysq** and press "return." The entry number, jobname, username, and status will appear. The job name is ACQ_FUND_NESTING_REPORT. The status is "pending."
- To reroute the job, type **setd** followed by a space followed by the entry number and press "return" (e.g., **setd 598**).
- To verify that the job has been re-queued and is running, type **draq** and press "return." This will show the entry number, jobname, username, and status on the DRA queue. The status is "executing." A message will appear across the computer screen when the job is finished. It usually takes just a couple of minutes for the report to finish.
- To print the report to the attached printer, select condensed print because the report is more than 80 characters wide. Then type **fnr** and press "return."

The report will look similar to the short example in Table 1: Fund Nesting Report in which numbers were rounded to the nearest thousand to simplify calculations.

TABLE 1. Fund Nesting Report

NEWTON GRESHAM LIBRARY
Fund Nesting Report
Sorted by: ID Start Date Type Owner Scope Class

Fund	Fund Owner	Total Allocation	Total Encumbered	% of Total	Total Expended	% of Total	Cash Balance	% of Total	Working Balance	% of Total
M-ASA-ART	010110	10000.00	3000.00	30.0	2000.00	20.0	8000.00	80.0	5000.00	50.0
M-ASB-SOC	010110	6000.00	1000.00	16.7	3000.00	50.0	3000.00	50.0	2000.00	33.3
M-ASH-ENG	010110	8000.00	5000.00	62.5	1000.00	12.5	7000.00	87.5	2000.00	25.0
Total		24000.00	9000.00	37.5	6000.00	25.0	18000.00	75.0	9000.00	37.5

The working balance is the field of most interest to selectors. It is the fluctuations in this field which selectors want to understand because it indicates how much money is remaining for new orders. Since this field is actually derived from a calculation using the allocation, encumbrances, and expenditures, factors which affect those three fields affect the working balance. In the next section, the key transactions which affect fund balances in the DRA acquisitions system are identified along with related acquisitions routines in the NGL.

KEY FUND TRANSACTIONS
AND ACQUISITIONS ROUTINES

In automated acquisition systems, there are key activities which result in fund adjustments. In the DRA system, when a purchase order is "placed," the funds are encumbered. When an invoice is "paid," funds are disencumbered and expended. When a cancellation report is "run with notices," orders are canceled and funds are disencumbered. Allocation adjustments can be made at any time but occur most often at the beginning and end of the fiscal year. Acquisitions routines which result in these key activities are the ones in which selectors are most interested. For example, how long does it take from the time an order is submitted until it is placed? When are invoices paid? How often is the cancellation report run? Detailed routines are described to show how the DRA acquisitions module operates. Suggestions for how the acquisitions department can inform selectors about the occurrence of the key transactions are discussed.

From the time selectors submit order cards to the time they are ordered, the following activities take place. Student assistants date-stamp the order cards with the date of receipt and check the public catalog to prevent ordering a duplicate copy. If essential bibliographic information such as the ISBN is missing, a search is done for that information. The cards are then sorted according to the vendor from which they will be ordered. For NGL's major vendor, Baker and Taylor, electronic inquiries are sent to verify availability of titles. Before adding titles to a purchase order, bibliographic records are added to the online catalog. This is done by uploading records from the Title Source bibliographic database or keying in short bibliographic records.

A staff member creates a purchase order in the DRA acquisitions system specifying the vendor, generating a purchase order number, and attaching the bibliographic records of the titles to be ordered. For each title, she specifies the list price, the expected discount, and the fund(s) to be charged. After all of the titles are added which are being ordered at that time from that vendor, the order is placed by typing "pl" at the appropriate screen. At this point, the estimated net cost (list price minus any discount) for each title is encumbered on its designated fund. For example, if the book *Sociological Methods and Research* has a list price of $50 with a 20% discount, $40 will be added to the current encumbrance field in the sociology fund. The purchase order is printed and mailed or, in some cases, e-mailed to the supplier. The order cards are filed by purchase order number in a small file drawer. Several orders are placed daily. From the time the order is received to the time it is placed varies depending on how much bibliographic information is on the order card, which vendor is selected, and other duties the library assistant is handling. However, an estimate of the average number of days is three to five.

Titles remain on order for varying periods of time depending on how long it takes the suppliers to send them. This can vary from as few as five days to a year or more. As the books arrive, student assistants open the boxes and check the invoices against the books. In the DRA "invoicing and receiving" module, an invoice header is created which includes the invoice number, invoice date, total amount of the invoice, and shipping and handling fees. Titles are added to the invoice header by a process which copies some of the information from the purchase order record to the invoice line item (e.g., the bibliographic information, list price, and discount). If the invoiced prices or discounts differ from the purchase order, they are corrected on the invoice line item. A receipt record is produced that shows the date and time the item was received. The funds are not adjusted until the invoice is paid by typing "pa" at the appropriate screen. Paying the invoice disencumbers and expends the funds and adjusts the cash balances and working balances. Several days may elapse from the time the invoice record is created until it is paid on DRA. This is due to the fact that, separate from the DRA system, the acquisitions department must complete paperwork required by the university's accounting system to initiate actual payment to the supplier. The university purchase vouchers are processed about once a week. While invoice receipt records are created on DRA on a daily basis, payment of the invoices on DRA is performed once a week to correspond with voucher processing.

Titles are canceled if they have not been supplied within the automatic cancellation period or the suppliers send notification that they cannot be obtained (e.g., out of print, no response from publisher, or publication canceled). Canceling orders in DRA requires running a cancellation report. This report is usually run about once every two weeks. It disencumbers money for the orders being canceled and readjusts the working balance. For example, if a biology book was encumbered for $100 and the order is canceled, the $100 is subtracted from the encumbrance which decreases the total amount encumbered for biology. The $100 is added to the working balance making it available for other biology orders. Some of the orders may be re-ordered from another supplier a few days after being canceled. Others are sent back to the selector after deleting the bibliographic record from the database.

CONCLUSION

The key activities resulting in fund transactions for most automated acquisitions systems revolve around placing orders, receiving or paying orders, canceling orders, and making allocation changes. The precise steps involved for the particular automated system in use is known by the acquisitions librarian and staff. The average amount of time it takes to perform some of these routines or the schedule followed may need to be better defined in order to be shared with selectors. There are time analysis studies that examine acquisitions workflow which provide ideas for conducting this type of research.[3]

There are other aspects of the acquisitions or fund accounting system that acquisitions librarians can share with selectors. In the DRA fund module, in addition to viewing the fund records online, the actual transactions for the funds can be examined. It may be worthwhile to demonstrate to selectors how to view encumbrance, expenditure, and allocation transactions. Selectors who are responsible for several funds can be given "inquire" level report privileges to run their own Fund Nesting Reports, if that format appeals to them. Selectors can be taught to check on the acquisition status of particular titles by looking in the public catalog. In DRA's public catalog, the status displays as "no holdings" for bibliographic records that are not in a placed purchase order. When orders are "placed," the status changes to "on order." When books are received and paid, the status changes to "received."

The acquisitions department in its role as service-provider should continually examine ways to meet the needs of its clients, in this case, the collection development specialists.[4] One of the needs of selectors has been to obtain fund accounting information on demand. With automated acquisitions systems it is now possible to fill this need by giving selectors authority to access fund information online. The responsibility does not end there. Online access requires that more information about acquisitions routines should be made known to selectors so that they will be better able to interpret the fund fluctuations they see online. This may require that the acquisitions department perform more self-evaluation and analysis of its activities than before online access was provided.

REFERENCES

1. Joyce L. Ogburn and Patricia Ohl Rice, "Service Through Automation: Sharing Fund Accounting Information," *The Acquisitions Librarian* 6: 149 (1991).

2. Karen A. Schmidt, "The Cost of Pre-Order Searching," *The Acquisitions Librarian* 4: 5 (1990).

3. Susan A. Cady, "Analysis of Technical Services Throughput on a Sample of Monographic Orders," *Technical Services Quarterly* 10(2): 17-27 (1992); Jeanne Harrell, Suzanne D. Gyeszly, and Jonie Gomez, "A Time Analysis of a Technical Services Workflow in a Representative Library: Year One Implementation of an Integrated System," *Technical Services Quarterly* 9(4): 49-61 (1992).

4. Ogburn and Rice, p. 150.

BIBLIOGRAPHY

Cady, Susan A. "Analysis of Technical Services Throughput on a Sample of Monographic Orders." *Technical Services Quarterly* 10(2): 17-27 (1992).

Harrell, Jeanne, Suzanne D. Gyeszly, and Jonie Gomez. "A Time Analysis of a Technical Services Workflow in a Representative Library: Year One Implementation of an Integrated System." *Technical Services Quarterly* 9(4): 49-61 (1992.)

Ogburn, Joyce L., and Patricia Ohl Rice. "Service Through Automation: Sharing Fund Accounting Information." *The Acquisitions Librarian* 6: 149-162 (1991).

Schmidt, Karen A. "The Cost of Pre-Order Searching." *The Acquisitions Librarian* 4: 5-20 (1990).

Cooperative Collection Development in PORTALS

Terry Ann Rohe
Patrice O'Donovan
Victoria Hanawalt

SUMMARY. Libraries are forming consortia and making commitments to cooperate. Librarians are using new computer technology to form the basis for cooperative activities and to communicate between libraries. The libraries in PORTALS have participated in projects including a serials weeding agreement, cooperative purchasing with matching grants, and a large-scale project to acquire more titles listed in the 1988 third edition of *Books for College Libraries*. This article discusses the possibilities and the drawbacks of these projects. *[Article copies available for a fee from The Haworth Document Delivery Service: 1-800-342-9678. E-mail address: <getinfo@ haworthpressinc.com> Website: <http://www.haworthpressinc.com>]*

KEYWORDS. Online reports, PORTALS, consortia, BCL3

Cooperative collection development is a cornerstone of resource sharing. It increases access to information and allows for the effective use of limited library resources. Libraries are trying to facilitate coop-

Terry Ann Rohe is Assistant Director for Technical Services and Collection Development at Portland State University Library, P.O. Box 1151, Portland, OR 97229. Patrice O'Donovan is the Linfield College Portland Campus Librarian, 2255 NW Northrup, Portland, OR 97210. Victoria Hanawalt is the College Librarian at Reed College, Portland, OR 97202.

[Haworth co-indexing entry note]: "Cooperative Collection Development in PORTALS." Rohe, Terry Ann, Patrice O'Donovan, and Victoria Hanawalt. Co-published simultaneously in *The Acquisitions Librarian* (The Haworth Information Press, an imprint of The Haworth Press, Inc.) No. 24, 2000, pp. 89-101; and: *Acquiring Online Management Reports* (ed: William E. Jarvis) The Haworth Information Press, an imprint of The Haworth Press, Inc., 2000, pp. 89-101. Single or multiple copies of this article are available for a fee from The Haworth Document Delivery Service [1-800-342-9678, 9:00 a.m. - 5:00 p.m. (EST). E-mail address: getinfo@haworthpressinc.com].

89

eration in collection management and development by sharing information and working jointly to increase the value of their resources.

Libraries across the country are making oral and written commitments to cooperate. They have formed consortia, purchased shared databases, and created electronic union catalogs. New technological means of assessment are providing tools for cooperative projects. Because they have better access to computers and better computers, library managers can now generate data that heretofore would have been unavailable. Vendors are offering to run electronic programs which match catalog databases to those of other libraries or to bibliographic lists. Although such programs are expensive to run, many libraries have chosen to have them done. The issue remains how the statistics are to be used. Can they be used in cooperative projects? How useful are they? Some recent Portland-based projects illustrate both the possibilities and the drawbacks of such efforts.

The Governor's Commission on Higher Education in the Portland Metropolitan Area (1989-1990) called for the improvement of information resources and services in the Portland area. The commission's report led to the formation of a metropolitan-area cooperative, led by a governing board of presidents of Portland institutions with substantial libraries. Planning for this venture began in 1991; a grant from the Murdock Trust supported formal planning in 1992. The charter for the Portland Area Library System (PORTALS)–a group of fourteen libraries of different types in the Portland/Vancouver area–was signed on July 21, 1993.

The goal of PORTALS is to "create the capabilities of an electronically accessible research library through shared resources of both public and private institutions."[1] The members of PORTALS are two public universities, one in Oregon and one just across the border in Washington, private colleges and universities, a community college, a multi-branch urban public library, and a historical society.

Charter Members:

Clark College, Vancouver, Washington
George Fox College (now George Fox University), Newberg
Lewis and Clark College, Portland
Linfield College, McMinnville
Multnomah County Library, Multnomah County
Oregon Graduate Institute, Beaverton

Oregon Health Sciences University, Portland
Pacific University, Forest Grove
Portland Community College, Portland
Portland State University, Portland
Reed College, Portland
Oregon Historical Society, Portland
University of Portland, Portland
Washington State University, Vancouver campus

Affiliate Members:

Marylhurst College, Lake Oswego
Mt. Hood Community College, Gresham

Governance of PORTALS consists of a Board of Directors (consisting of the Presidents and CEOs of the member institutions), a Council of Librarians (the library directors), and an Executive Director. Standing committees have been established to address such matters as interlibrary loans, access to electronic databases, and collection development.

The Cooperative Collection Development Committee was formed with the mission of reviewing a collection assessment provided by the Western Library Network and making recommendations to the Council about how to proceed with cooperative collection development.

COOPERATIVE PROJECTS

One of the first cooperative projects among the PORTALS libraries was a serials weeding agreement. On December 16, 1994, a group of representatives from PORTALS libraries met and planned the implementation of this agreement. If a cooperating library is considering withdrawing a serial run or canceling a serial title, and if the title is the last or next to the last copy in the area, that library must notify other member libraries before taking action. Other libraries may approve the action, recommend reconsideration, offer to subscribe, or offer to house the items to be withdrawn. The agreement was reviewed after eighteen months. Responses to the project were positive. A number of libraries had exchanged material based on notification. The ability to transfer our lists to e-mail from a word-processing program makes it easy and inexpensive to notify other institutions of withdrawals and cancellations. Items can be transferred via a courier already under contract for document delivery in Oregon and Washington, so shipping materials is not difficult or costly.

Another cooperative project grew out of a $10,000.00 fund established by PORTALS to help build on the collection strengths of PORTALS libraries. Proposals were requested from member libraries on how they would use these funds. The awards were partial matching funds–two-thirds supplied by PORTALS to be matched by one-third from the participating library. The grant funded the acquisition of materials which had to be one-time purchases and had to be available for circulation among PORTALS libraries. These purchases were to build upon the strengths of PORTALS member collections and had to fill a documented need.

As an example, Portland State University Library and Reed College Library applied for $3,043 to purchase 436 biographies from a local book collector. They agreed to match this money with $765 from each library. The seller, well-known in Portland as the former owner of a bookstore, had spent many years developing a fine collection of biographies, most of them of literary figures. The subjects include hundreds of well-respected writers, including James Agee, Dante, George Bernard Shaw, and Wordsworth. This collection was checked against the holdings of the Portland State Library, the Reed College Library, and the Multnomah County Public Library. Duplicates were eliminated from consideration for purchase. When the grant was awarded, the volumes were distributed evenly between the two libraries with the help of one librarian from each institution and several faculty members. The collection will support historical and literary research throughout the city and will benefit the entire community, including high-school students, college and university communities, independent researchers, and general readers.

In a larger project, PORTALS contracted with the Western Library Network in 1994 for an electronic collection analysis and received four reports:

(1) In the collection analysis report, the classification number from each bibliographic record was matched with a corresponding conspectus line number, counted by occurrence and reported by division and category levels. PORTALS was shown to have 1,744,528 discretely held titles among items cataloged in machine-readable format. This count would be considered a mini-

mum. Not all of the PORTALS libraries had completed retrospective conversion, so the actual number of discrete titles was understood to be higher.

(2) The gap analysis compared PORTALS titles with those at the University of Washington. The report listed titles held by the university but not by any library in PORTALS.

(3) The title overlap report identified uniquely held titles and shared titles. Unique titles are those that only one library owns. These numbered 840,222.

(4) The fourth report compared the bibliographic entries in the 1988 third edition of *Books for College Libraries* (*BCL*) with the holdings of the PORTALS libraries. *BCL* lists approximately 50,000 titles recommended as part of a basic collection for libraries serving four-year undergraduate institutions. A list of *BCL* books not held by any PORTALS library was produced. Another printout listed items which appeared to be close to the *BCL* listing, but could not be matched exactly using only electronic means. Exact matches occurred for 91.3% of the titles in *BCL*. Since Portland State University, the largest library in the system, had not finished retrospective conversion, the "miss" list and "close match" list were both checked against the PSU card catalog, a process which produced many more exact matches on pre-1976 imprints.

The PORTALS Cooperative Collection Development Committee began by gathering bench marking information on how such data were used by other libraries or consortia throughout the country. In May, 1994, Sally Loken of WLN provided a list of libraries that had used the matching service. This list included the Rasmuson Library at the University of Alaska, Fairbanks, the Merrimack Valley Library Consortium in Massachusetts, Montana State University Library, Boise State University Library, Gonzaga University Law Library, Gonzaga University's Foley Center, and North Seattle Community College Library. Librarians at those institutions were contacted by telephone and asked how they had made use of the data, which information was most helpful, and which projects were most fruitful.

THE BCL3 PROJECT

After comparing the efforts of other institutions and considerable discussion, the committee began work on a project in which all titles indicated as misses on the *BCL* list would be purchased if they were judged to be of potential interest to any PORTALS library. Twelve member libraries agreed to participate in the project. The Committee used statistical sampling to determine the best way to discover the level of commitment a library might have to various subject areas. The Committee assigned purchasing areas based on the collecting statistics available through the WLN matching project. While retrospective strength of particular collections was a factor in determining assignments, a library was given responsibility for a subject area only if it was shown to be still actively collecting materials in that discipline.

In the fall of 1995, each participating library was sent printouts generated by the WLN automated matching project representing the list of non-matches, a list of the subject headings that they had been assigned, and a set of guidelines for the project.[2] Participants were asked to review the lists and reject titles they recognized as no longer essential. For instance, they may have been aware that a book published later which was already in their collection contained better information than the title listed in *BCL*. There were cases in which more current or accurate research materials were available and older items were deemed to have little use for historical research.

We expected that a number of the books would be out-of-print, but urged participants to try to obtain them on the used-book market if they were still deemed valuable.

The project was comparable to that of the nineteen academic libraries in Montana, which was described by Mary C. Bushing in the *WLN Participant*.[3] WLN provided a *BCL* match for the libraries in 1992; they were shown to have 83% of the titles listed. The libraries made a commitment to increase their holdings to at least 90% by means of a cooperative project.

PORTALS libraries participating in our project were asked to review their statistics by the end of July, 1996, and report to the committee on the progress they had made. Three committee members studied preliminary reports submitted in the summer of 1996. A final institutional report covering acquisitions activity through December 31, 1996 provided the data summarized in Tables 1 and 2.

TABLE 1. Activity by Institution

BCL PROJECT

Institution	Titles Assigned	Titles Ordered	% Ordered	Titles Received	% of Ordered Received	Total Spent	Spent/ Title
Clark College	149	31	21%	22	71%	$1,152	$ 52.36
George Fox University	157	133	85%	35	26%	1,657	47.34
Lewis & Clark College	383	77	20%	48	62%	1,779	37.06
Linfield College	338	174	51%	100	57%	3,217	32.17
Multnomah County	434	379	87%	113	30%	5,727	50.68
Oregon Graduate Institute	83	7	8%	7	100%	770	110.00
Oregon Health Sciences University	102	24	24%	21	88%	822	39.14
Pacific University	131	105	80%	18	17%	655	36.39
Portland Community College	197	148	75%	83	56%	2,857	34.42
Portland State University	636	530	83%	147	28%	6,510	44.29
Reed College	464	404	87%	121	30%	11,316	93.52
University of Portland	398	114	29%	88	77%	5,553	63.10
SUMMARY	3,472	2,126	61%	803	38%	$42,015	$ 52.32

REACTIONS TO THE BCL3 PROJECT

The request for a final report from individual libraries included the following open-ended statement, "We would like to ask that you share your reactions to the project–what was good about it, what was negative, what you perceive as possible outcome. Please share anything you think would benefit someone reading about this project and considering undertaking a similar project." Anonymity of respondents' reactions was guaranteed.

All participating libraries did provide final statistics, but only about 60% went the next step to record their reactions to the project.

The responses addressed three principal issues: first the process of the project, especially difficulty encountered in trying to purchase out-of-print books, second the value of the materials purchased, and finally the perceived value of having participated in this consortial project.

The final report included the following reactions to the process:

"It is somewhat disappointing to realize that the Library was able to obtain less than fifty percent of the titles on the lists. This percentage might have been higher had we the resources to pursue out-of-print titles more vigorously using a variety of sources. Given the staff constraints we relied most heavily upon [a local bookstore] or our regular jobbers to obtain out-of-print materials."

TABLE 2. Activity by Subject

Subject Area	Titles Acquired	Spent		Spent/Title
Agriculture	21	$1,064	(est.)	$50.67
Anthropology	4	106		26.50
Art/Architecture	17	862	(est.)	50.71
Biology/Medicine	21	822		39.14
Business/Economics	50	2,883		57.66
Computer Science	1	80		80.00
Education	11	718		65.27
Engineering	53	4,609	(est.)	86.96
Geography /Earth Sciences	14	538		38.43
History	11	363		33.00
History–Africa	26	743		28.58
History–Asia	36	2,293		63.69
History–Canada	7	352		50.29
History–Europe	48	2,328		48.50
History–Latin America	6	321		53.50
History–U.S.	34	1,723	(est.)	50.68
Lang/Lit	17	698		41.06
Lang/Lit–American	81	1,472		18.17
Lang/Lit–Classical	9	303		33.67
Lang/Lit–English	79	8,029	(est.)	101.63
Lang/Lit–French	56	3,617		64.59
Lang/Lit–German	15	1,429		95.27
Lang/Lit–Italian	2	19		9.50
Lang/Lit–Provincial/Colonial	29	436		15.03
Lang/Lit–Russian, E. European	21	683		32.52
Lang/Lit–Scandinavian	5	154		30.80
Lang/Lit–Spanish/Portuguese	9	320		35.56
Library Science	10	428		42.80
Mathematics	1	65		65.00
Music	5	216		43.20
Performing Arts	15	563		37.53
Philosophy	19	953		50.16
Political Science	29	1,244		42.90
Psychology	2	76		38.00
Religion	24	939		39.13
Sociology	15	566		37.73
TOTAL	803	$42,015		$52.32

"The final list was unclear, in some cases, as to whether titles were owned within PORTALS libraries. This caused some unnecessary double-checking of titles."

"It was . . . fair to the smaller and more specially oriented libraries for two reasons: first, they agreed voluntarily to participate and second, they could reject any titles they didn't want to buy."

"The acquisitions section found this to be an annoying project because so many items were out-of-print or hard to obtain. They did not question the worth of the additions to the collections, however. We expect that in other libraries there will have been some grumbling over the request to purchase some older titles, but that is why librarians were asked to review the lists and eliminate titles they felt were no longer useful."

"On a cost/benefit ratio, the amount of staff time spent on the project is not balanced with the quality of the addition to our collection."

"The data received to work from was very poorly produced and annotated; few instructions or explanations of holdings at other libraries were received."

"*BCL* listings were incomplete and inconsistent–few had ISBNs; publisher information was sketchy. A high percentage of the listings are out-of-print."

"For every subject area, I found that we had ownership of some of the items beyond and above those noted."

Comments on the value of the materials purchased included these remarks:

"In looking at what we have ordered and thus far received, some of the titles seem a bit esoteric for our collection. It would seem that the value of such a project will be truly as PORTALS intended, as part of a regional collection, rather than merely elements within a single library's holdings."

"The older books are worth more for research in areas such as the humanities and social sciences than in the sciences. We were happy to purchase many of the older titles, but librarians rejected a number of books because they were no longer current and some other better resource had been published since."

"We felt that the addition of one copy of many of the older titles to the holdings of the Portland area made the project worthwhile."

"For a [library] such as ours, the *BCL* titles were out of scope. Although a reasonable attempt was made to give [us] responsibility for titles within our scope, the titles assigned were not."

"The *BCL* titles were very dated, especially for our academic setting. Many titles dated back to the 1970s."

"The question was raised by several staff that, if the books in *BCL* were of high quality, why hadn't the college libraries in PORTALS purchased them in the first place?"

"I think this was a worthwhile project. It was a good cooperative project in that it focused on a standard/recognized set and it was relatively easy to divide responsibilities among institutions. It assures (to the extent that it is possible) that a collection of recognized academic titles are somewhere in the consortium. There were some limitations in that *BCL* is somewhat dated now, and many books are out-of-print and/or perhaps not very relevant."

"I think the *Books for College Libraries* project was almost worthless. Most of the books were out of print, and it seems, if they weren't purchased originally, they must not have been all THAT great. Also many, if not all, of the books were out of date, with newer, better books written in the interim . . . a more recent edition of *Books for College Libraries* (had it been available) would have made more sense."

"I question just how useful the purchased items will be to POR-TALS users."

"Whether adding these titles was worth the substantial costs involved (particularly in terms of staff time) is questionable."

Comments on the value of participation in the project included the following:

"It was good that a cooperative project was put together and implemented. I think this was a very worthwhile project."

" . . . as a pilot project in cooperation it was worthwhile, because it required the various librarians from various institutions to think and act cooperatively, avoiding duplication."

"We participated in the project to cooperate in the building of a virtual library in the Portland area and to create a sense of goodwill among participants. The value of the additions to our collection for our users, specifically, and for PORTALS members in general, was secondary. The main benefit of the project for [our library] will be to have demonstrated a willingness to participate in a cooperative collection development process among diverse PORTALS libraries."

CONCLUSION

In conclusion, the reactions of the majority of respondents noted the difficulty in obtaining out-of-print items. Many questioned the value of the items to their own home libraries, but felt that there may be a benefit to the consortium as a whole.

There was near total agreement that participation in the project was in itself the most valuable outcome. It demonstrated that the various types of libraries could work together cooperatively on a project. The majority of participating libraries felt that the general goodwill, the feeling that all had worked together as a team, was important and of great value, even though the worth of some of the actual titles added to the collection was questioned.

An important feature of this project was that members contributed their own funds to support it.

It is likely that our success rate would have been much better if we had had access to the kind of out-of-print search capability that has recently become available via the web.

A logical next step might be to review circulation statistics of the books that were purchased both in home libraries and as interlibrary loans among PORTALS members. Portland Community College Library reported that among the eighty-three titles they acquired, forty-one circulations occurred by the beginning of November, 1997. A general review of circulation data is not planned at this time.

Assignments for this and other projects have not required member libraries to make permanent commitments to collecting responsibilities in subject areas. A more formal and long-lasting division of collecting responsibilities would involve many issues that did not arise with these projects.

NOTES

1. *PORTALS Portland Area Library System*. (Portland, OR: PORTALS, 1992).
2. *PORTALS* Cooperative Collection Development Committee. *Books for College Libraries* (*BCL*3) Project.
3. Bushing, Mary C., "Montana Academic Cooperative Collection Development and the WLN BCL3 Service," *WLN Participant* (May/June, 1993): 12-14.

GUIDELINES

Books for College Libraries (3rd edition, 1988), a project of the Association of College and Research Libraries, constitutes a "recommended core collection for undergraduate libraries."

PROJECT GOAL

To insure that every appropriate title cited in *BCL*3 is held by at least one PORTALS library. This project is to be completed by December 1995.

POLICY ISSUES

I. Project Participants: All 14 member libraries will be offered an opportunity to participate in this project, but participation is not required.

II. Current *BCL* Holdings: For purposes of this project, holdings in the collections of all institutions which were part of the WLN assessment will be considered as contributing to the goal of the project. Thus, non-member library holdings also will be counted as matches in the *BCL* project.

III. Titles to be Acquired: On the assumption that *BCL* lists materials desirable for any basic academic collection, the goal is to acquire 100% of the missing *BCL* titles. Exceptions may be made for dated materials, textbooks, or earlier editions of individual titles. The library charged with filling in holdings in a particular subject area will have the discretion to exclude individual titles if they are judged not to be of potential interest to any PORTALS library.

IV. Collecting Responsibility: The library with responsibility for filling in titles in a particular subject area of *BCL* will be selected based on an assessment of established strength in a given area, combined with a current commitment to developing collections in that subject. Assignment of collecting responsibilities will be recommended by the Cooperative Collection Development Committee and approved by the Council of Librarians, and are intended to apply to this project only.

V. Ownership and Access: Titles added to a library as part of this project will be considered to be owned by that library, but subject to the resource sharing agreements which are the foundation of the PORTALS network. All titles acquired as part of this project will be fully cataloged by the owning library and available for loan to other PORTALS libraries.

VI. Weeding Guidelines: Participating libraries agree to make reasonable efforts to retain last copies of titles listed in *BCL*3, or to offer such titles to other PORTALS libraries before weeding them.

VII. Funding: Libraries which assume collecting responsibility for *BCL* titles in a particular subject area will purchase these materials using their institutional acquisitions budgets. Each library will maintain records of number of titles purchased and amount spent on this project.

PORTALS will assume responsibility for costs related to reproduction of assessment forms and other related expenses.

PROCEDURAL ISSUES

I. Non-matches: Titles for which no match was found in the tape comparisons conducted by WLN will be checked by PSU against its holdings when the non-matches are pre-1976 publications in classifications which have not yet undergone retrospective conversion.

II. Close matches: Titles which were listed as close matches will be reviewed to determine if these items should be considered to be held by PORTALS or should be treated as non-matches and added to the list of titles to be acquired.

III. Out-of-Print (OP) titles: It is estimated that roughly 50% of the titles in *BCL* may be out of print or available only through reprint publishers. The goal of acquiring *BCL* titles will include OP items unless they are excluded by the criteria outlined in #3 of the Policy Issues.

IV. Acquisitions procedures: Each library assigned responsibility for filling in particular subject areas will acquire titles through normal institutional acquisitions procedures.

Online Management Reports:
A Book Vendor's Perspective

Scott Alan Smith

KEYWORDS. BNA, online reports, vendors, books

Earlier this year Will Jarvis invited me to contribute an article to *The Acquisitions Librarian* on the subject of online management reports, and I happily agreed to do so. As I began to think about what to say on the topic, and how to go about saying it, I reflected on the book trade's recent history and the development of some recent trends. Hence I decided to start with a bit of an overview of where we've been, in order to put the matter of where we are and where (I think) we're headed into context.

First, though, I should say that my views are the product of a fairly specialized segment of the market: I've spent my career to date selling books to academic libraries. Although much of what follows grows out of that experience, I think it will prove applicable to the market at large. Moreover, while I'll focus primarily on book vendors, there are many parallels to the services of periodicals agents.

A BIT OF BACKGROUND–DATA MISSED

Although books–and bookdealers–have been around for centuries, book vendors specializing in the supply of books and related products

---

Scott Alan Smith is Regional Sales Manager, Blackwell's Book Services, P. O. Box 14650, Portland, OR 97293-0650 (e-mail: scott.alan.smith@blackwell.com).

[Haworth co-indexing entry note]: "Online Management Reports: A Book Vendor's Perspective." Smith, Scott Alan. Co-published simultaneously in *The Acquisitions Librarian* (The Haworth Information Press, an imprint of The Haworth Press, Inc.) No. 24, 2000, pp. 103-107; and: *Acquiring Online Management Reports* (ed: William E. Jarvis) The Haworth Information Press, an imprint of The Haworth Press, Inc., 2000, pp. 103-107. Single or multiple copies of this article are available for a fee from The Haworth Document Delivery Service [1-800-342-9678, 9:00 a.m. - 5:00 p.m. (EST). E-mail address: getinfo@haworthpressinc.com].

103

to academic libraries are a much more recent development. A great deal has already been written about the Richard Abel Company, so I'll keep my opinions brief. Abel did several significant things, two of which merit mention here: he was the first modern wholesaler to recognize academic libraries as a unique market (and subsequently developed many products and services specifically for them), and he was a pioneer in automating vendor operations.

Up until the 1960s, bookdealers (and libraries) operated in a manual environment. Libraries typed orders and mailed them to vendors; vendors in their turn typed purchase orders and mailed them to publishers. When books were pulled from inventory or received from publishers, invoices were typed and sent with shipments to libraries. Unless someone took the trouble to compile a lot of data by hand, reports detailing speed of supply, overall fulfillment, or other aspects of vendor performance were simply unavailable. As a result, there were few reports–and little demand for such information.

As support for higher education increased in the 1950s and 1960s, book budgets grew and libraries ordered more books. Larger budgets attracted the attention of vendors; hence the sixties saw substantial growth in the number of people, and companies, serving the market.

Increased volume meant greater stress on the manual procedures common to the industry at the time, and the advent of mainframe computers promised efficiencies beyond the scope of those manual procedures. More volume also meant more profit, which helped finance the considerable expenses involved in the development of the computer systems of the day.

The process of automating vendor operations continues today. As is true for most industries we are constantly upgrading and replacing systems, and the introduction of PCs, networks, the internet and the Web have had, and continue to have, a profound effect on our internal systems, and the products and services we offer our customers.

AUTOMATION–DATA FOUND

For our internal operations, vendors focus on three important components: the books themselves, the publishers we buy them from, and the libraries we sell them to.

Before we automated we depended on printed resources for information about what titles were in print, how much they cost, and other appropriate information (e.g., is the title in a series?). To improve our ability to track the very product we sell, we set about creating and maintaining bibliographic databases.

Where and how to buy are critical questions as well. Knowing that a given imprint has been sold by publisher A to publisher B influences where we send our orders–so the creation and support of a publisher file comes into play.

Once we've got the books, we have to know what to do with them: who ordered this title? How is it to be invoiced? How do we ship to this customer? What special instructions, if any, should obtain in handling this order? Hence our need for a customer file.

Ideally these files interact in the context of a larger system. We need inventory control, financial management to deal with our accounts payable and accounts receivable (as well as other, non-book trade specific functions, like payroll), and other basic business capabilities.

For the purpose of this article, though, it's those three aforementioned components that are important. The data we gather and maintain on books, publishers, and libraries gives us the ability to generate management data, both for our own use and for the benefit of our customers.

PRINTED REPORTS

The advent of vendor automation made possible a range of status and management reports now common to the industry. Now, when a book vendor learns (and confirms) a particular title is out-of-print, it's a simple matter to dispatch status reports to every client who has an outstanding order for that book.

Many vendors have also developed standardized management reports. These reports usually provide information on number of books supplied within a given period, list and net prices, and appropriate performance statistics. Most often these reports reflect the segmentation that's become commonplace to the trade: we talk of firm orders, approval books and notification form titles, and standing orders.

Such reports are generally supplied according to a regular schedule of the library's choice; on demand; or both. While there are several options for date range, format, and content, some limitations exist.

Firm order reports are usually provided to assess service. What's the vendor's overall fulfillment? How quickly are orders filled? What percentage of orders are cancelled or reported out-of-print?

Approval plan reports can be divided into three categories: (a) reports detailing sales activity, (b) reports tracking profile performance (i.e., approval book return rates; or forms usage statistics), and (c) industry-wide information on title output and pricing trends.

Reports for standing order customers typically identify volumes supplied against specific series; reflect title changes, or information on titles that have merged, split, been completed or discontinued; and publication history.

These reports have become a common part of our industry's vocabulary, enabling clients to assess service levels, plan budget allocations, and manage approval programs with efficiency and precision. With the development of vendor online capabilities, the possibilities for more highly-tailored, on-demand reports increase substantially.

THE ONLINE REPORT–GREATER FLEXIBILITY

Online access by libraries to vendor's files opens a new realm of possibilities for management information. Not only can librarians now request a broader range of reports, but in addition such reports can be more directly tailored to the users' needs. The ability to specify exact date ranges; combine separate and several sales types; and determine report formats are all features that emerge as vendors bring more resources to bear on the delivery of management information.

By now "online access" and "web access" are almost synonymous. Most major book vendors have home pages, and increasingly these Web sites are more than merely "virtual brochures." Access to bibliographic resources, online ordering capabilities, and interactive account maintenance are increasingly commonplace.

What does this mean for management reports? Greater flexibility and immediate delivery of information.

Moreover, a new generation of management reports is emerging. Approval plan customers have for many years utilized reports detailing sales and returns data to target areas of their profiles that may require revision. Reports on the use of notification forms (or approval slips) have also been used to identify profiles that might be upgraded to automatic shipments.

Increasingly, approval customers can view their profiles on the

Web, and can model suggested profile revisions to see what consequences these changes would introduce. Let's say your library has had
an approval plan focused on university presses, and you want to examine
the viability of adding selected trade publishers. Perhaps you're also
considering the addition of some subjects that have not hitherto been part
of your plan. By crafting a provisional profile online, and matching it
against bibliographic data for a given historical period (e.g., the last fiscal
year) you can view the number of books and their associated costs. You
can then compare the results to the same data for your existing profile,
and decide whether the changes render acceptable results.

In addition, the ability to generate multi-institutional reports is being
given consideration by several vendors. Such reports can be very useful
for cooperative collection development efforts, either by working to
dovetail different libraries' approval profiles, or by targeting selective
series for acquisition by cooperating institutions.

WHERE TO FROM HERE?

Dramatic change continues to confront the academy, and librarians
are compelled to address an increasingly fragmented world. Tight
budgets, price increases for traditional materials (especially periodicals), and demand for many new formats (video, CD-ROM, docu-
ment-delivery, etc.) make the task of library acquisitions an ever more
difficult one. Moreover, attrition and re-allocation of staff mean that
many libraries now have a much smaller technical services staff, and
very often librarians with responsibility for collection development
are obliged to share this job with a burgeoning array of other duties.
Hence the need to manage acquisitions and collection development
functions becomes ever more essential. The use of online management
reports available from vendors, in conjunction with the reporting capabilities of local automated library systems, is likely to become so
necessary as to become commonplace. Look for greater sophistication
of both vendor and ILS offerings, as well as increased interface options between such systems. Demand for these features is also certain
to increase.

All of this presupposes, of course, that libraries will still be buying
books in significant numbers. For both personal and professional reasons, I for one earnestly hope this proves to be true.

Claiming in the Automated Environment

Sarah D. Tusa

SUMMARY. This article discusses the role of automation in journals claiming and explores ways of monitoring the effectiveness of claiming in the automated environment. Discussion covers the differences between using automated claims and system-generated claim reports and the possible implications of each for managing the claims work flow. Lastly, the article examines the experiences of serials managers who responded to a survey regarding claiming practices and results with the use of automated claims and claim reports. *[Article copies available for a fee from The Haworth Document Delivery Service: 1-800-342-9678. E-mail address: <getinfo@ haworthpressinc.com> Website: <http://www.haworthpressinc.com>]*

KEYWORDS. Serials, claims, claiming, online reports

It is a generally accepted precept that the purpose of automation is to enable better service to library users. In the serials environment, better service is largely defined as more efficient access to information materials, which in turn requires effective management of serials control databases–such as check-in and claim records. In their effort to achieve better management of their journals collections, serialists have implemented automated serials control modules, either as components of an integrated library system (ILS) or as stand-alone systems. When one considers the importance of serials control to the support of re-

---

Sarah D. Tusa is Assistant Professor, Serials Acquisitions Librarian, Mary & John Gray Library, Lamar University, LU Sta Box 10021, Beaumont, TX 77710-0021.

[Haworth co-indexing entry note]: "Claiming in the Automated Environment." Tusa, Sarah D. Co-published simultaneously in *The Acquisitions Librarian* (The Haworth Information Press, an imprint of The Haworth Press, Inc.) No. 24, 2000, pp. 109-116; and: *Acquiring Online Management Reports* (ed: William E. Jarvis) The Haworth Information Press, an imprint of The Haworth Press, Inc., 2000, pp. 109-116. Single or multiple copies of this article are available for a fee from The Haworth Document Delivery Service [1-800-342-9678, 9:00 a.m. - 5:00 p.m. (EST). E-mail address: getinfo@haworthpressinc.com].

search and curricula and the substantial amount of financial and human resources that libraries invest in these materials, it becomes very clear that every effort must be made to extract the fullest possible benefit from automation in the area of serials control. Assessment of current performance is vital to the successful development of ever more effective serials control modules. If automation is to be truly beneficial to serials control, it must go beyond routine check-in to facilitate management of some of the more problematic aspects of journals. One such case is claiming.

As Marcia Tuttle has astutely noted: "Claiming missing issues and volumes is one of the most time-consuming and neglected aspects of serials acquisitions."[1] Since missing issues constitute a gap in our ability to provide timely access to information materials, it is crucial that serials automation modules provide the means for effective and efficient journals claiming. With the advent of library automation systems, serials management has indeed seen substantial innovation. For example, most automated serials modules provide some form of predictive check-in, and are capable of generating automated claim reports or electronic claims. Some systems provide the capability of either of these two functions. The immediate benefit of such claiming functions should be more effective claiming. That is to say, missed issues should be detected more promptly than with manual systems; hence, claims are placed in a more timely fashion, and the fill rate improves. With so many publishers placing narrow time limits on the claims they will honor, it is becoming increasingly more important to detect and claim errant issues as promptly as possible. When automation facilitates prompter and more accurate claiming of skipped or late issues, it enhances the serials manager's ability to provide ready access to journals for students and researchers. In the interest of assessing the extent to which library automation is serving this purpose, it is important to assess the efficacy of the claiming functions of our automated systems.

One of the few documented efforts to assess the relative value of claiming in an automated environment was provided by Judith Rieke, who reported on her staff's experience with the use of a vendor's online system to generate and send claims.[2] This study compared the amount of time it took to process online claims, compared to the time required to prepare manual claims. It also compared the response time for online claims to that of manual claims. Rieke summarizes that it took longer to process online claims, but that in the end, online claiming was preferred because it resulted in prompter responses from the vendors and prompter receipt of journal issues.[3] Now that more serials modules are part of an ILS and are more fully integrated with the check-in function, it is time to reexamine the benefits of automated claiming. In addition, new questions must be posed to begin an up-dated and comprehensive assessment. While it is beneficial to attain a faster response time for claims, it is also desirable and reasonable to expect a higher fill rate. Moreover, to be deemed truly efficient, auto-mated claim reports should also serve to streamline the claims work flow, requiring less time rather than more.

In order to examine the relative success rate of claims before and after implementing the serials module of the ILS in use at the Mary & John Gray Library, I extracted claims statistics from the annual reports of the past ten years. Since we had transferred the majority of our active journals from the manual system to the automated system by the end of fiscal year 1992/1993, said year serves as the dividing line between the two sets of statistics displayed in Tables 1 and 2. This dividing point also marks a substantial increase in the percentage of claims filled that year, as compared to the previous fiscal year 1991/1992. Contrary to my expectations, however, there have been generally fewer claims per year generated since implementing auto-mated check-in than were issued on the average in the previous five years. In fact, an average of 696 claims per year were sent to vendors and publishers from FY 1987/1988 to FY 1991/1992, while the aver-age number of claims issued in the succeeding five years fell to 337.2. On the other hand, the percentage of claims filled rose by nearly sixteen percent in the years following implementation of the serials module. This comparison would appear to indicate that automation has indeed led to increased effectiveness in claiming, but there are other questions to be considered when assessing the overall progress of claiming in the automated environment.

TABLE 1. Claims Statistics Prior to Automating Journals Check-in and Claiming

Fiscal Year	1987/88	1988/89	1989/90	1990/91	1991/92
No. of Claims	970	511	850	582	567
No. of Claims Filled	444	298	378	271	313
Fill Rate	45.8%	58.3%	44.5%	46.6%	55.2%

TABLE 2. Claims Statistics After Automating Journals Check-in and Claiming

Fiscal Year	1992/93	1993/94	1994/95	1995/96	1996/97
No. of Claims	474	370	303	279	260
No. of Claims Filled	382	222	173	179	188
Fill Rate	80.6%	60%	57%	64.2%	72%

In order to enable the most efficient and effective claiming possible, automated claim functions must identify late issues accurately. Depending on whether one uses claim reports (otherwise known as late notices) or automated claiming, the immediate effects of inaccurate claiming differ somewhat. In the case of electronic claiming, the system produces a claim that is mailed or electronically transmitted to the publisher or vendor. In such cases there is limited opportunity for the serials staff to intervene in the process. While in many instances it is possible to exert some indirect control over such claims by making adjustments to the respective check-in records, this can be a labor-intensive and continual procedure. If there is sufficient time, staffing, or opportunity to make necessary adjustments–for delayed issues, numbering anomalies, etc.–the system or module may generate premature claims. Serials managers must be perennially on their guard in this respect, since, "according to Frank Clasquin, publishers estimate that 50 percent of library claims are premature."[4] Such inaccurate claims have been known to invoke unpleasant telephone calls and correspondence from publishers. More importantly, these false claims ultimately undermine the integrity of communications between the serials staff and the publisher, which situation in turn can lead to having legitimate claims disregarded and thus unfilled.

In the case of system-generated late notices, the serials manager does have the opportunity to review those titles designated as late before issuing an actual claim. It has been the experience of this author, having worked with three different automated systems, that the lists of late issues generated by the respective serials modules are unjustifiably long. To give an approximate, but no less indicative, image of the problematic efficiency of automated late notices, I compared the number of late issues listed on three separate claim reports with the number of actual claims determined to be legitimate for each list. The results are displayed in Table 3, which represents

TABLE 3. Results of Reviewing Claims Reports for Issues Listed Prematurely

Date of Claim Report	Number of issues listed for claiming	Number of issues rejected for claiming	Percentage of issues rejected for claiming
11/01/1995	208	46	22%
02/01/1997	207	14	6%
02/02/1998	211	4	1.9%

activity from three somewhat randomly selected monthly claim reports from 1995, 1997, and 1998.

While it is true that the majority of missing issues listed on each of these reports were cases legitimately requiring claims, there are sufficient numbers of premature listings to warrant continued manual review of the claims reports, though these numbers appear to be retreating. Those potential claims eliminated from the final claims list are generally issues that were received within ten days after the claims report was generated, or issues for which the system incorrectly estimated an issue date and/or expected date. (Since I noticed this tendency fairly soon after implementing the current serials module, I have made it a practice to wait approximately two weeks before processing each claim report.) Unlike Rieke's study, our staff has not recorded or monitored the amount of time required to review the claim report or to translate them into actual claims, but it generally takes four to five hours to check the individual titles listed against the database to ascertain which issues actually need claiming and which would constitute premature claims that should be omitted from the list. Although we are getting a better fill rate for our claims, as documented earlier in this paper, the amount of time required to adjust the serials database, combined with the necessity of thoroughly reviewing the claim report, renders the efficiency of claims less than satisfactory. This observation led me to wonder about the experiences of other serials managers who are grappling with the claims process.

In the interest of initiating dialogue and promoting further research on the evaluation of serials claiming functions in automated environments, I conducted an informal survey via the Internet. Thanks to the courtesy of the Serialist listserv, the survey was distributed to the targeted audience of serials or journals managers from a broad geographic expanse. The responses to the survey reveal an array of practices in regard to the monitoring of claiming efficacy and the efforts to enhance the performance of automated claiming. The survey included the following questions:

1. Is your serials module a stand-alone, or part of an integrated system?
2. Does your serials module feature automatic claiming and/or late notices?
3. Do you use: (a) automated claims, or (b) automated late notices?
4. In what year did you implement your current check-in module?
5. Do you keep claims statistics?
6. If the answer to #5 is "yes," have you documented an increase or decrease in claims generated since you implemented automated check-in?
7. For those who keep claims statistics, has the fill rate for claims increased, stayed about the same, or decreased since implementing automated check-in?
8. Does your library keep statistics on how many Interlibrary Loan borrow transactions are generated by missing issues? If so, can you document an increase or decrease in this type of ILL activity for your library since automating your serials check-in?

Of the thirty-nine respondents, only six reported they are currently using stand-alone serials check-in modules. This number is too small to provide a meaningful comparison with the responses from those with integrated systems, but the input from the stand-alone users contributes to the overall estimation of the efficacy of automated claiming, which was the general purpose of the survey.

The second and third questions of the survey were perhaps too ambiguously worded to elicit the kind of statistics that were the intended result. In asking whether the system in use features automatic claiming and/or late notices, I had hoped that respondents would specifically indicate which of the two functions their respective system supported, or whether it supported both functions. At least half of the respondents replied "yes" to this question, but did not indicate which of the three possible claiming situations described their systems. What I had hoped to determine from the collated answers from this and the subsequent question was whether there was a marked preference among serialists in using one method or another, where there was a choice. Of those who clearly indicated that their systems featured both automated claiming and late notices, no such preference was evident. However, a few respondents who chose to use system-generated late notices did specifically comment that they perceived a need to check the claim letters or lists against their periodicals shelves and check-in records before forwarding an actual claim to the publisher or vendor. It is further revealing to note that of the thirty-nine respondents, twenty-two indicated that they use either late notices or a combination of late notices and automatic claims. Nine respondents indicated that they use the automatic claims function alone. Two respondents indicated that they use neither of these functions.

The most startling finding of the survey is that the majority of those who completed the survey reported that they do not keep or record statistics that are vital to monitoring the performance levels of their serials modules in regard to claims. Of the fifteen serials managers who did indicate that they keep claims statistics (Question #6), only eleven were able to answer questions #7 and #8. Since over one-third of the respondents indicated they have implemented the serials module they currently use as recently as 1995, it is perhaps understandable that they have not yet found it meaningful to compile such statistics, especially if they are still making adjustments to the module or to the records therein.

Of those who did answer questions #7 and #8, a slight majority indicated increases in the number of claims made since automating their serials check-in. However, while eight respondents reported that the number of claims made in a year has increased since automation, only six reported that the fill rate has improved.

It is important to note, as did a few of the librarians who completed the survey, that there are several factors that can influence the relative success or failure of claiming. One serials manager specifically pointed out that while she is not satisfied with the fill rate for her claims, she attributes the poor responses to certain publishers. Another serials manager was quite explicitly displeased with the performance of her vendor in handling claims for her library. More detailed statistics would be required to support either position. Allowing for the existence of these and other external factors, there are nevertheless some features in serials check-in modules that can make a substantial difference in the level of success one can attain in filling gaps in current journals holdings.

For example, most of the serials managers who reported satisfactory claim results also indicated that they were able to adjust either an action interval or an expected date of receipt in order to avoid erroneous claims or late notices. The ability to manipulate key components of the online serials database helps primarily because computers are designed to count with ruthless accuracy and consistency, while the publication schedules of many journals defy any pretense of regularity. Even journals with seemingly regular publication patterns are often prone to delay or irregularly combined issues that confound the serials module's limited capacity for guessing.

The purpose of the last question of this survey (#8) was to raise awareness of the impact that missed journal issues have not only on researchers, but also on the workflow of other departments, such as Interlibrary Services. Unless local policy prohibits, gaps in journal availability are generally compensated by use of this department, which also frequently serves as the library's document delivery outlet. Despite the fact that telefacsimile technology has enabled 24-hour turnaround for delivery of articles, the extra steps needed to obtain this material for the library user is an added encumbrance that effective claiming should be able to minimize. Continued design improvements in serials modules, such as increased flexibility in check-in patterns and better methods of issue prediction, should in turn further enhance the usefulness of automated claims and claim reports in the constant vigil against journal service gaps.

Clearly, further studies are required in order to fully assess the extent to which automation is meeting its potential for rendering journals claiming more efficient and successful. The purpose of this paper has been to examine some of the ways serials managers can begin to question the efficacy of their serials modules with regard to claims, and to identify some of the obstacles to maximizing the benefits of automation for the purpose of filling or preventing gaps in the library's journal holdings. By assessing the current efficiency and effectiveness of automated claiming functions and by ascertaining which barriers need to be overcome by better software design, serials managers can suggest meaningful improvements to their ILS vendors that will contribute to enhanced fulfillment of the purpose of automation in the library.

REFERENCES

1. Tuttle, Marcia, Managing Serials, Greenwich, CT: JAI Press, Inc., 1996. [Foundations in Library and Information Science, v. 35.] p. 173.

2. Rieke, Judith, "Online Claiming: What Benefits?" *Serials Review*, 14 (3), 1988, p. 20-31.

3. Ibid, p. 31.

4. Tuttle, p. 182. See also: Frank F. Clasquin, "The Claims Enigma for Serials and Journals," in *Management Problems in Serials Work*, edited by Peter Spyers-Duran and Daniel Gore (Westport, CT: Greenwood Press, 1974), p. 76.

Evolution of the INNOPAC:
Managing Resources
with Statistics and Reports

Sandra Westall

KEYWORDS. Management information, millennium, INNOPAC, on-line reports

Does having an automated library system guarantee you will get the management information and statistics that you need? Not necessarily. Only a system that has been designed with management needs in mind will provide the wide range of needed reports.

Managing resources is an important component of library technical service operations. Effective resource management requires information about resources and their usage. Knowing which materials are in demand; knowing which parts of the collection are strong or weak; knowing how far the financial resources have been spent and encumbered; knowing price increase patterns–these are all examples of the types of information necessary for effective resource management. Statistics and management reports are the supporting data necessary to make informed decisions.

Integrated library systems provide the potential to store and gather great quantities of data–far more than could ever be tallied or counted

Sandra Westall is Vice-President and Director of Reference Database Services, Innovative Interfaces Inc., 5850 Shellmound Way, Emeryville, CA 94608.

[Haworth co-indexing entry note]: "Evolution of the INNOPAC: Managing Resources with Statistics and Reports." Westall, Sandra. Co-published simultaneously in *The Acquisitions Librarian* (The Haworth Information Press, an imprint of The Haworth Press, Inc.) No. 24, 2000, pp. 117-123; and: *Acquiring Online Management Reports* (ed: William E. Jarvis) The Haworth Information Press, an imprint of The Haworth Press, Inc., 2000, pp. 117-123. Single or multiple copies of this article are available for a fee from The Haworth Document Delivery Service [1-800-342-9678, 9:00 a.m. - 5:00 p.m. (EST). E-mail address: getinfo@haworthpressinc.com].

117

by hand. Along with the ability to collect, data can be coupled with programs that present the data in logical and meaningful reports. These reports should be a natural extension of the ILS basic functions, such as sending a purchase order.

Useful management reports don't happen automatically. Advance planning and design is required to make sure that data is stored in ways that the data can be retrieved and manipulated. As systems grow and features expand, new types of reports and new types of data must be part of the program design.

When the INNOPAC system started out as an Acquisitions-only INNOVACQ system in 1981, the system was envisioned as a management tool as much as a production tool. In the very earliest release, a number of financial management reports were available. As the system has evolved into the integrated INNOPAC system with a variety of modules, the management reports have been an integral part of development. Now, as INNOPAC heads into the INNOPAC Millennium, one of the first development products provides management reports in Web-based, JAVA run applications. Existing reports have been given added functionality while new reports provide more extensive statistics.

FROM INNOVACQ TO MILLENNIUM

For the very earliest INNOVACQ, design requirements were included to provide a broad range of management reports. These included: funds able to be grouped in hierarchies with the system supplying subtotals and totals; vendors analyzed for performance; new acquisition lists generated easily and sorted in any desired order; and up-to-the-minute reports on funds over- or under-spent. Reports were available both online and in hard copy.

As INNOPAC evolved, many additional reports and statistical capabilities were added. These included the ability to compare expenditures during one fiscal period to another and have the system predict the future fiscal needs based on past history. Fiscal comparisons were originally available across funds, vendors, or other codes. The evolution of this capability was then extended to provide predictions by title–especially useful for journal titles where multiple years of fiscal history are retained.

One of the most powerful management tools in the INNOPAC is the report generator, known as the Create Lists function. This function allows libraries a tremendous flexibility to find subsets of records within the system. Any field, whether indexed or not, may be searched. Coded fields may be searched by codes, variable length fields may be searched for strings of characters, and numeric fields searched for greater/less than specified values. Search arguments may be combined using Boolean operators. Thus it is extremely easy, for example, to find all the records which have payments made within a specified time period and which cost over a specified amount. The resulting subset of records may be used for a variety of purposes, including statistical reports.

The INNOPAC provides a statistical function that generates a number of statistical reports on demand. These include counts by coded data elements within the records; cross-tabulations involving two selected fields; and classification counts, which can also include dollar amounts spent within call number ranges. The reports can be run over a range of records or over a previously determined set of records.

Millennium Web management reports represent the newest evolution of management information. This module delivers the rich management information already available in the character-based INNOPAC and extends it with reports and cross tabulations previously unavailable. The convenience and power inherent to retrieving management reports via a Web browser make it even easier for library staff to pull out needed information on demand, and there is the added ability to produce colorful, graphical reports in print form–pie charts as well as bar graphs and tables.

Web displays and Java programming offer the opportunity to expand far beyond what was previously available in character-based online displays. With a Web display, the data is no longer restricted to a 24 × 80 black and white screen. Data can be displayed in different size fonts. Colors can enhance and define displays. Graphs and charts can offer different visual representation of statistical data. Java applets can provide the programs to draw the charts and to provide calculations. See Figure 1.

With the Web-based reports, an entire new suite of collection management reports has been added. This includes comprehensive, integrated statistical reports which correlate data across the various modules of cataloging, acquisitions, and circulation. For example, there is a report that tabulates data such as average payment per order, per call

FIGURE 1. Pie-Chart Representation of Library Budget

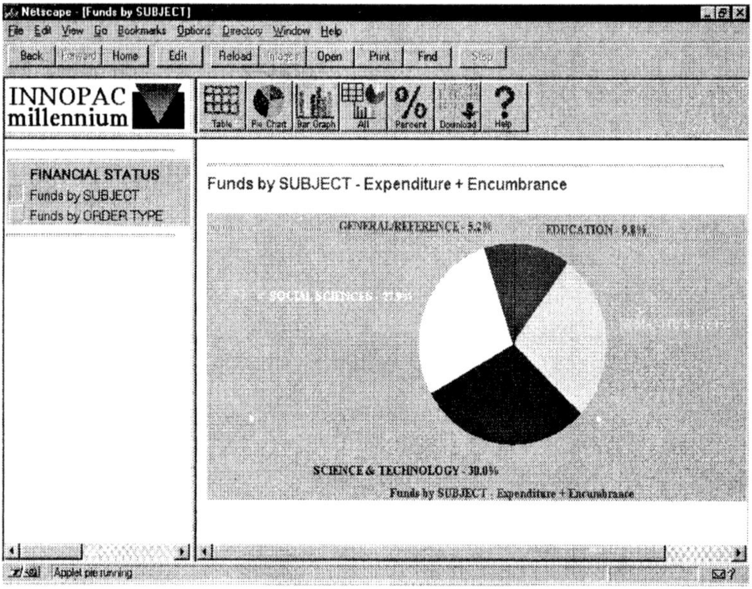

number classification, correlated by the number of circulation check-outs for the same classification, and computes the average acquisitions cost per circulation. See Figure 2.

As new modules are developed for INNOPAC, new management reports are integrated into the development. For Electronic Reserves, Web-based management reports contain information about the number of times each article is retrieved online or printed, with reports cumulated by publisher. For the Web Access Management module, Web-based reports contain information about the number of times each server is accessed and breaks the access down by time and patron type.

The INN-Reach consortium software, which provides patron-initiated circulation among multiple systems, provides a number of reports with valuable information about which sites are borrowing from others, with cross-tabulations between sites for requests, fulfillments, and cancellations. The system also calculates a lender/borrower ratio, so it is extremely easy for a manager to determine which sites are net

FIGURE 2. Collection Development Report Cross-Tabulating Collection Size, Acquisitions, and Circulation

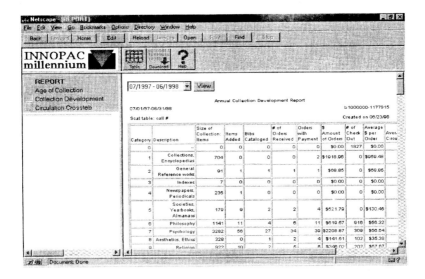

lenders versus net borrowers. Additional statistics record the patron types that are performing requests, while other statistics record the number of available items to which the patron had access when the request was made. See Figure 3.

DESIGN AND PLANNING

Integrated systems support huge volumes of activity across a number of modules. To provide good management reports, facts about these activities must be stored in ways that can be both retrieved and manipulated. Any one activity, such as a circulation checkout, will require that several pieces of transaction data be stored, such as: date, time, patron type, item type, call number classification category, shelving location, and other relevant codes about the patron and item. All this data must be stored efficiently since it can consume a significant amount of disk. The data should also be cumulated in ways that make retrieval and calculations easy and relatively quick. Management reports cannot be easily tacked onto a system at a later time if

FIGURE 3. INN-Reach Statistics for Fulfilling Patron-Initiated Circulation Among Multiple INNOPAC Systems

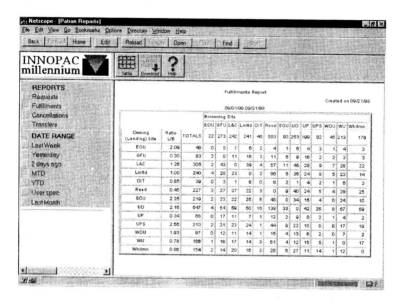

early planning does not accommodate the storage of transaction data. If the data does not exist, there is no way to include it in a report, and no amount of programming can produce reports if there is no data.

Librarians' needs include easy to use reports with lots of data. At the same time, librarians want the flexibility to create that "special report" that is so critical to their library. Ease of use and flexibility are not always compatible design issues. A report that is canned and just pops up on the screen may not contain the desired data. However, having great flexibility requires more expertise in formulating and using statistical reports. To accommodate the varied needs and skills of the librarian users, the INNOPAC provides a variety of reports. Some, especially those that analyze large quantities of data, are predetermined and offer the user a set number of options for how the data can be arranged and displayed. Other programs allow the user to create their own reports, using tools to find relevant data and statistical packages to analyze that data. With the new Web-based Millennium reports, data may also be exported as a delimited file. These exported files may then be imported to spreadsheet programs where the data can be manipulated even further. This newest capability combines easy access to data with the added flexibility of using data in customized ways.

Many criteria should be considered when evaluating a system's ability to produce statistics and reports, including:

- Quantity of data
- Quality of data
- Ability to cumulate and analyze data
- Flexibility to retrieve and manipulate data
- On-line displays
- Printed reports and ability to export
- Ease of use
- Speed

Not all of the above criteria are compatible with each other at the same time, which leads to a variety of methods and reports. Statistics and management reports are among the added-value benefits possible with automated systems. An array of such reports is even better. Good system design will provide the breadth and quality of reports needed for informed decision-making.

Coordinating Report Functions from Online Systems: A Philosophic Essay

William E. Jarvis

SUMMARY. A pragmatic design-analysis philosophy of online management report features and functions is articulated for the efficient and useful compilation of all kinds of synoptic and detail-oriented online reports. Principles, practices, and possibilities are expounded for acquiring, assembling, analyzing, and appraising online management reporting features and functions. A variety of the many reports which library managers could acquire from various online library systems and applications are considered. The twin indexing and cataloging concepts of precoordination and postcoordination are used here to characterize a methodology of designing, utilizing, and comparing management report features from online sources. This subdiscipline of library-information science is defined by the author as "reportology." This essay is *not* a comprehensive survey of the particulars of downloading information into microcomputer applications, of mainframe "plumbing" report specifications, or a compendium of management report features found in various ILSs. (Some INNOPAC examples are featured, however.) Rather it is a sort of "philosophical primer" utilizing some analyzed cases-in-point of management reports, which are examined from the perspectives of hybrid informational media, complex library organizations, and increasingly powerful technical-functional capabilities. *[Article copies available for a fee from The Haworth Document Delivery Service: 1-800-342-9678. E-mail address: <getinfo@haworthpressinc.com> Website: <http://www.haworthpressinc.com>]*

William E. Jarvis, Librarian 3 (Associate Professor level), is Collection Services Librarian, Washington State University Libraries, Pullman, WA 99164-5610 (e-mail: jarvis@wsu. edu).

[Haworth co-indexing entry note]: "Coordinating Report Functions from Online Systems: A Philosophic Essay." Jarvis, William E. Co-published simultaneously in *The Acquisitions Librarian* (The Haworth Information Press, an imprint of The Haworth Press, Inc.) No. 24, 2000, pp. 125-154; and: *Acquiring Online Management Reports* (ed: William E. Jarvis) The Haworth Information Press, an imprint of The Haworth Press, Inc., 2000, pp. 125-154. Single or multiple copies of this article are available for a fee from The Haworth Document Delivery Service [1-800-342-9678, 9:00 a.m. - 5:00 p.m. (EST). E-mail address: getinfo@haworthpressinc.com].

125

KEYWORDS. Post-coordinated, pre-coordinated, philosophy, INNO-PAC, ILS, review article, hybrid formats, online reports, enhancements

INTRODUCTION

I have been very interested in the functionality of specifying and obtaining management reports for over 15 years of collection management work. And although I have published on aspects of this vast subject, I have not previously carried out a general philosophic treatment of the area (Jarvis, 1991, 1992). Many fundamental aspects of acquisitions/technical service systems functionality, including some basic evaluations of management report capabilities, have been outlined in the past, most notably by Boss (Boss, 1982, 1992).

What is, and is not, being regarded here as a "management report"? Any "report" of interest to a "manager" can, of course be (and probably has been!) called a management report, somewhere by someone. An individual module's record screen in a system can readily be excluded from a management report definition, but not much else can categorically be ruled out of at least potentially being a "management report." Since almost any data can be of value to a manager at one time or another, and especially since the emphasis here is on the need for the easy, efficient compilation of report data from online library application system sources, an exclusive definition of "management reporting" is of little value in and of itself.

(Even the "simple" matter of labeling "a single ILS record" with its complex relational database format of bibliographic-order-item-serials checkin records by using some single inclusive term may not be readily doable.) Calling such a whole ILS record set a "bibliographic" record set can lead to confusion when an Acquisitions client is interested in a variety of record fields of an ILS record set other than the solely MARC bibliographic facet. Perhaps the unwieldy term "ILS title record set" could serve until something short and sweet comes along. Conversely, a "non-title," "holder-record-ILS record set" consisting of such record types as fund-vendor-patron-course reserve records (in INNOPAC again) also lack adequate linkage descriptions. It is rather curious how the whole ILS complex of a single title's inclusive set (a.k.a. the "full" ILS book record) and even the added associated, non-title records such as fund record, vendor record, patron record, course reserve record resist an easy, short designation.

These definitions matter due to the often trans-record-based character of creative online report gathering operations.

This paper is not intended to serve as an encyclopedic treatise (comprehensive or concise) about online management reporting features. Rather this essay is a reconnaissance of the "terrain" of the state-of-the-art of online reporting. And as in any good reconnaissance we will be concerned with what is going on now as well as what is coming up "ahead" of us. The treatment of particulars in this study is more of a collection of "snapshots" from a variety of perspectives than a comprehensive treatise-type "Handbuch." The definitions implicit in the cases reviewed throughout this volume are sufficient to delineate this fuzzy-set, ever-changing pragmatic field of study.

I have coined the term "reportology" to cover this subdiscipline of library-information science and practice. Perhaps a phrase such as "report function and features studies" would be more precise, but the use of a single word to group these philosophic and pragmatic studies is convenient, even if the term used is "reportology"!

If books and other "library materials" bear a "second-order" relationship to reality/existence/professional operational practice, and indexes/reports are thus "third-order" relationships to library materials, then "reportology," the study of online report-features can be said to be a "fourth-order" activity. Reportology is then indeed a very abstract library science subdiscipline!

Extensive experience with and contemplation of online report design and use has led me to the following basic generalizations about online management report needs, namely the importance of the twin cataloging/indexing concepts of "pre-coordination" and "post-coordination." Look over the other papers in this collection and see if these twin coordination notions have any applicability to the situations described in them. Also, then look at your own library agency's management information reporting practices in the light of the pre- and post-coordination continuum as well.

Many aspects of librarianship can best be seen through the looking glass of online management information reports. My own recent tasks at the workplace are a good case in point. In early 1998, for example, I was working on projects such as:

- Potential modifications in WSU's BNA book-approval shipment profile settings, utilizing both the Blackwell's *Collection Manag-*

er website and certain as-if printouts with potential yield rates of proposed profile modifications.

- Training/orientation of other library faculty in such management information areas as fund reports, lists of order records by type, and a variety of statistical reporting features.
- Exploring with other WSU library faculty what organizational approaches to tasking personnel to carry out management information capture and analysis.
- ILS enhancement recommendations for our INNOPAC ILS Management Information "module's" report features.
- Working out export and storage of key ILS archival report data outside of the ILS domain, i.e., in a network-type share file environment.

All of these examples are commonplace online management reportology concerns of many librarians in a variety of roles: collection managers, acquisitions librarians, technical service administrators, budget officers, and library directors.

"Precoordination" and "Postcoordination":
Toward a Philosophy of Reportology

These twin concepts of precoordination and postcoordination are very useful in analyzing online report functionality. These twin concepts have long been used in the realm of cataloging and indexing but have not heretofore been systematically defined and used to analyze online report writing features and functionalities, although they have been commonly utilized in library science indexing courses over the years.

LCSH-type indexing is of course a classic exemplar of precoordination. DIALOG/ERIC-type descriptor Booleanation is an example of postcoordination. "Keyword in context" (KWIC) and "Keyword out of context" (KWOC) are also familiar distinctions closely related to the notions of precoordination and postcoordination respectively. In general, postcoordination tends to be a more inclusive search rubric than precoordination, both in the indexing field and in online management reportology. LCSH precoordinated indexing terms such as subheadings can, of course, be "KWOC-ed" in a rotated descriptor display fashion and even Booleanated in a postcoordinated fashion. The rigorous application of this spectrum of coordinating schema can often clarify existing online report functionalities, and also inform our developmental approach to possible new design features and options. However, just like so many other overarching conceptual schematics, absolute "Aristotelian" either-or logical parsing of messy contingent realities is not always possible (or desirable) due to the myriad pragmatic limitations inherent in human creations such as integrated library systems. Aspects of any one-report feature can, of course, sometimes be seen as mixes of both precoordination and postcoordination, sort of on a sliding scale between two pristine extremes.

Precoordination and Postcoordination in Management Reporting Design Philosophy: It has been observed that, "An automated system should be expected to yield or produce statistical and other management reports" (Corbin, 1985). How do we as library professionals get our online statistical, record list and other management reports?

Borrowing the indexing terms "precoordination," i.e., Key-Word-in-Context (KWIC), LCSH-type hierarchical subject index access and "postcoordination," i.e., Key-Word-out-of-Context-type (KWOC), non-hierarchical subject index access) can assist in sorting out some major differences in management report design philosophy. A do-it-yourself selection of data-elements from various systems by downloading them has considerable appeal and makes a virtue out of necessity in many circumstances. While it also provides considerable freedom for library sites to gather reports from their system-configurations, postcoordinated downloading can also shift work onto library staff. It can also shift the responsibility for good reporting features and easy online report-writer features especially, away from automation vendors. ARL sites, for example, all have by definition a need for standard, annual statistics. Systems should provide these in canned, classic precoordinated fashion. Reports should not have to be laboriously assembled in a miscellaneous fashion by a costly postcoordinated download set of procedures. All libraries want at least year-by-year price increase data, by title and by fund. All libraries also want current average data, if they can readily get them. Most libraries welcome dense spreadsheet-like arrays of fund and order statistics rather than, for example, merely a one-fund-per-printout-sheet report form displays. If we are to have vendor reports, library acquisition module reports, or parent accounting agency reports, why should they often need to be routinely reformatted onto PC-based spreadsheets just to get such standard stock-in-trade products as percentiles, averages, or even just to get easy-to-compare closely set columns? Why can't we readily get the data we need in the form in which we need it, whatever systems "progress" is made? See, for example, Carrigan's very informative survey (Carrigan, 1996).

PC- "Refereed" Data Entry in Payment Code Errors and Collection Level Volume Counts: One way to do such postcoordination is via a system download to a PC-based application. A classic use of the PC-based spreadsheet as an "umpire" of multi-system fund flow error detection occurred in a newly configured GEAC 8000 Acquisitions system many years ago. A bookkeeping data entry error occurred when a constant data function lead to several incorrect payments codes being incorrectly assigned. Monographic monies disencumbered correctly and expended correctly on the Library side, while the separate financial services code on the University/parent agency side of the GEAC accounting subsystem simultaneously registered an incorrect expenditure against the global subscription account on the University side of the Acquisition systems' accounting categories. Because the spreadsheet data for each smaller departmental cost center fund was copied (manually) off the disencumbered library side of the expenditure double entry, the audit trail was relatively easy to follow and fix. Without spreadsheet data driven using the less fallible department sized funds, this error would have been hard to detect. Although it showed up readily in the "Library" side grand fund balances vs. the "University" side GEAC 8000 Acq fund balances, it was the spreadsheet data that simplified the troubleshooting. That dual entry GEAC 8000 fund structure did not prevent the error, although it did display the unequal balances (Jarvis, 1988).

However, a PC-based template doesn't always "receive" such a downloaded overlay perfectly, for example, if the ILS dataset's zero value(s) don't export as a zero cell in the PC application's data column. (It's happened to me, I know.) In my case the spreadsheet data consisted of collection holding volume counts by LC Class-range (Jarvis, 1989).

The importance of PC-based management reports concept could-should grow if the idea of acquisitions modules as part of bibliographic integrated library systems weakens. Post-activity coordination of management-relevant fund data would still be important to trackers of average prices, detailed cost center departmental funds, and encumbrance data. Conversely, if the joint "gravitational" pull of vendor and parent organization payment/accounting systems remains weaker than the strong linkages of library-centered, bibliographic integration of systems, the acquisitions modules could–should–be reducing the role of microcomputer-based postcoordinated manipulation of fund data. The acquisitions (and other) ILS modules should anticipate and fulfill more of our fund management reporting needs in either a precoordinated, in-the-can report formats, or in a report writer postcoordinated with the ILS approach. The INNOPAC Management Report module is one example of such a flexible, built-in report writer facility.

Rationale for the High Precoordination of Uniform Reporting Requirements in Online Library Systems: In 1993 WSU Libraries carried out a Management Report Task Force project to identify necessary and possible management reports data and statistics. At the time, the Libraries contemplated internally co-developing a new in-house integrated library system. Thus the desiderata list developed by the Task Force was envisioned as the (RFP-like) specifications for the management information "module" of a to-be-developed integrated library system. One of the watchwords of the Task Force members, and of the parent WSU Libraries Database Coordination and Implementation Committee, was that data and formatted reports should be readily collated by the integrated library system. For example, that Committee reasoned that since virtually every library in the U.S. has an entry in the *American Library Directory*, why not have a full data set preformatted to produce just such statistical entries for that *Directory* each year, rather than manually compiling data piecemeal? Obviously, even with such fairly "canned" statistically laden entries as those of the *American Library Directory*, the way those different libraries can and do vary reporting data to a degree. So such optional "postcoordinated" configurations would be best built into ILSs as variable settings and formatting. No checklist will probably ever perfectly match the operational groupings of a system's functions. Rather, such checklists are merely sounding boards for the possible recording of what a system can do (and can't do!). See, for example, Appendix C for a 1993 checklist collated by that Task Force.

For example, it's become a "standard obstacle" for quantitative analytic measures such as the endeavors of the North American Title Count Subcommittee to find that potential participants often do not have canned or even readily "report-writable" LC Class volume-tallying capacities available within their current online systems (ALA

North American Title Count Subcommittee discussion, 1997 and ALA Program, 1998).

Non-fund accounting acquisitions statistics, order statistical inventories, are fairly standardized in our profession. Why don't all Acquisitions (and other) modules give their users densely arrayed reports automatically saved on a set frequency, i.e., monthly, basis?

"Hybridology": The Challenge of Integrating Online Management Reporting in an Era of Paid-for Multi-Access

An assumption: The ongoing management of access and ownership in the library realm is now and will fundamentally remain a hybrid process, at least for the foreseeable future.

Employing the logical dictum of "Ocam's Razor" (not multiplying entities beyond necessity) several corollaries can be drawn for acquiring online management reports for library decision support, statistics counts, and lists of record-types. Whether the need is to fund account departmental cost-centered program support being carried out by a mega-periodical full text data set, the collating of fund balance reports from a variety of vendor-based acquisitions utilities, or the justification of the percentage of document delivery support to an academic teaching department chair, there is an increasing need to track with reports a hybrid and even "dis-integrated" acquisitions/management information environment (Ray, 1993).

Balanced against this potential array of hybridized access sources and acquisition system utilities is the difficulty of maintaining a stand-alone spreadsheet application such as *Lotus* or *Excel* to record the looming welter of fund account monitoring on such a PC-based stand-along spreadsheet. Anyone who has tried to maintain a detailed spreadsheet and reconcile it with one or more Acquisitions ILS-module-based reporting features knows how two accounting systems can "wander away" from each other, like two (or three!) children with a parent in a park. All the standard caveats regarding the need for frequent budget justifications pertain in the increasingly hybridized world of multi-sourced online reports.

Is it possible to continue to integrate all library-land fund-reporting needs (with meaningful data) in a single "automatic" encumbrance and expenditure transaction-based reporting system, like that found in several turnkey integrated library systems? If not, then our emerging mix of document delivery and Internet full text serial title sets will rapidly fragment more and more of our detailed fund reports, leading into an increased irrelevancy for our "traditional" ILS-base fund report structures.

Hybridization is not only a continued regard for a *decreasing percentage* of traditional print media vs. online formats, or even the *persistent presence* of the potentially "dis-integrating" "gravitational pull" of the systems of material vendors and controllers financial offices on libraries ILSs, but also an *increasing hybridization* as multiple paid for access, sources and various online modalities multiply in libraries and fragment our fund, collection, and other management report capabilities.

INTEGRATED COLLECTION MANAGEMENT IN "HYBRID," "VALUE-ADDED" ENVIRONMENTS

Collection management coordination is a value-added activity by virtue of its management activity, as well as due to its involvement with new high-tech sources and traditional material format's high prices.

1. Coordination of collection development–including overall coordination, coordination with other collection management activities, such as preservation, serials management, etc.
2. System coordination of collection development with online systems, ILS, vendors, etc.
3. Since the basic reality is that a hybrid mix of electronic and non-electronic resources is the prospect for the indefinite future, balancing the use of, and "accounting" for both in an integrated way is paramount. (We must both do good and tell our clients "how good we did"!)
4. Statistics: of "haves," of "wants," Collection Analysis, Collection Level Assessments, Combined Usage Studies, i.e., circulation (by patron type and by LC Class) vs. Acquisitions Level. Is there a moral to all this? Collection management, including Acquisitions work, not only manages valuable sources, but can itself be a value-added service, if the coordination of people, systems, sources, and statistics is done well.

Reportology Coordination: The Organizational Front

On the "organizational front," let's consider work group functioning and also the desirability of a "wide-portfolio" reports coordinator type of position responsibility in libraries. A pivotal concern of group dynamics and professional coordinating is the massive degree of complexity inherent in report work.

Possible Functions of a Library's "Statistical Working Group": It seems very desirable for a library to have a management report or statistics working group to adequately take advantage of the many possibilities of contemporary ILS statistical/reporting features. Such groups could for example carry out these closely related activities:

1. Advanced study/information-sharing about the complexities of ILS reportology.
2. Specification of usage/enhancement prospects for the future.
3. Assist various consumers in their data-gathering/interpretive efforts.
4. Team-teach introductory, intermediate, and advanced in-service classes.
5. Coordinate the review of the various modules' report-featured codes in the ILS.
6. Develop suggestions to contribute to evolving organizational needs and uses of the whole range of management information and statistical features.

Level of Complexity Required in Reportology Expertise: However, having stressed here the value of a statistical team of coordinating professionals, one wonders how many people can realistically master complex search strategies and the semi-documented "ritualistic procedures" of executing ILS list report and statistical searches, especially if the searcher uses the features only 1-2 times a year at best. For example, one can even email a saved search strategy from say INNOPAC to another library person, but learning or remembering the rationales or factors regarding such a strategy can be problematic for the occasional user. An INNOPAC Create List example, which I was using the other day to get a serial quote list ready, is a case in point. See, for example, Figure 1: "Paid date AND Fund code range."

Remembering referencing the fund code structure for the whole range of serials, filed designations, command conventions, fixed field

FIGURE 1

"Paid date AND Fund code range example from INNOPAC Release 11":

SEARCH STRATEGY 10: "wsujarvisSER-G7/96-SIE-12":

<FUND between 11000 & 19000
AND PAID DATE > = 07-01-96 >

codes for subscriptions ("s"), continuations ("i") or electronic serials ("e"), and the implicit nesting Booleanation conventions for INNO-PAC searching (always putting OR's at the end) is only the beginning of a long "liturgy" of online processing to reach a full report product.

Codes such as "s," "i," "e" are single letter code designations which each INNOPAC site can define. At WSU these were our choices. Other sites might of course vary these conventions. The initiation of a library organization into a full functional use of an ILS's management reporting features is itself a human management challenge, since the complexity of a library's organizational culture has a multiplicative effect when coupled with the complexity of the contemporary ILS. And there is no sign that ILS design is getting simpler–to the contrary! Multiply "feature-accretion" across the many modules of an ILS can make a full technical appreciation of a full ILS record-set virtually a whole course of graduate study. Would-be users of cross-module report-relevant code-values face these challenges daily.

"Management Information Services Librarian" Positions as Potential Coordinators of Reportology Throughout a Library and Its Systems: It is my position here that the coordination of online management information report features and sources (at least in larger libraries) can best be done by a position solely dedicated to that vast array of work.

One possible solution is for larger libraries to designate a full time "Management Information/Reports/Statistics" coordinator, with wide report-gathering/writing responsibilities. See Appendix A for a sample position description. Among the beneficial outcomes could be:

- Coordinating the management information and collection management needs of library administrators, collection development divisional heads, Library Council, and processing staff. (These needs and the potential for meaningful applications to address them have grown with our increasing budgetary needs and our implementation of the INNOPAC system here.)
- Long-term institutional flexibility in collection management coordination and ILS-based management information studies

could be maximized by such a proposed professional role which could contribute essential value-added management lists and statistical information and coordination in libraries would be enhanced.

A library need not be wedded to any one job role title: variant title possibilities include: "Collection Management Information Services Librarian," "Collection Management Information Coordinator," "Collection Management Information Services Librarian," "Management Information Services Coordinator," or "Collection Services Coordinator." Although some of these duties might currently fall under the rubric of a collection development officer in many organizations, not every possible automated and organizational system-wide tasks and assignments would necessarily fit into the collection development mold.

Focus on Statistics Issues in Collection Development Management: We must count what we have and what we want in as many ways as needed. Otherwise we cannot properly justify what we've done, are doing, or want to do.

- Utilize ILS-produced data and statistical "report writing features" whenever possible.
- Recognize that statistical reports, whether ILS-derived or not, can be described in a continuum ranging from "pre-canned" to virtually "ad hoc" in composition.
- Statistics, while not an end in themselves, are a vital means of leverage. With good statistics we can get good collection management.
- Collection management statistics need to encompass electronic copyright access as well as print ownership-based copyright-access: this includes fund reports.
- New system RFP processes are a "golden opportunity" to prepare desiderata of statistics of all sorts.
- The "report writer" and "hard-wired" statistical features of an ILS are a very, very important matter to consider when picking a new system.

Some Suggested INNOPAC "Management Information" Enhancements

I believe it is a valuable theoretical and pragmatic exercise for a report coordinator to systematically critique the ILS or systems they work with as to the usefulness of that system's online report producing capabilities. I should stress at this point that INNOPAC is a very powerful, very complex ILS. It is also the contemporary system I know best. (Two of the three previous acquisition systems I have worked with do not exist anymore, which is an interesting point for any library manager to reflect upon from time to time!) So INNOPAC is just serving here as a convenient example for purposes of illustration.

This section is a critique of some features of INNOPAC "reportology," focusing on file storage and user-friendly, occasional complexities: For example, here are three things INNOPAC doesn't provide, and thus requires storage outside of the INNOPAC server environment:

1. Full sort and strategy storage for Statistics searching and sorting.
2. Limited search strategies and Created List file space in INNOPAC Create Lists.
3. *No* INNOPAC file saves for Created Statistical Reports at all.

Solution: Park these archive lists and data sets outside the INNOPAC domain, in a shared networked PC-type share-file storage. Note Figure 1 above, consisting of the first screen (of many!) that illustrate 5 stages in preparing a management report product, only one of which (saved search strategies) is automatically, fully recorded within the ILS.

"Syndetic" Relationships Among Various Order and/or Other Types of ILS Records: One enhancement aborning for the INNOPAC Integrated Library System is a 1997-balloted enhancement which enables one Order record to be linked to a multitude of Bib records, thus facilitating Order and various downstream processing and tracking. If every online syndetic, cross-referencing, relationship is a management report feature, at least potentially, in a subsequent-to-occurrence "create list-able," later report-type fashion. (Conversely, some online syndetic "cross-reference" relations are essentially instantly "real-

ized online report groups.") These online syndetic relationships are a sort of instant quasi-management report feature.

Operating the online system, with its "one-minute" realized syndetic structural functions, is the acquiring of the online management report. For example, the goal of keeping track of what's going on is what management reports are for.

There will be no attempt here to articulate or permutate the many order-type designations possible. Suffice it to say that there are numerous options (all?) of them *very* system dependent, as to how order typology can suffice. Order-types could conceivably serve both as the detailed fund accounts number (by departmental cost center type of accounting breakout) and as the traditional "what kind of order is it?" (form-approval, book-approval, firm-order, continuation series volume) designator. Order types could be used, for example, to designate a form-approval set of books and also whether that book is a biology departmental cost center item; provide that enough order type terms are available.

A second e-feedback opportunity into the ILS is the publisher-status "report-back." Claim responses and OP availability quotes are areas of opportunity. The current X.12 standard of online serial issues claiming sends out to vendors but does bring in the response. The library and vendor worlds have not yet realized the operational state where a library's ILS can routinely receive a publication-status input from a material vendor for an outstanding order record *the day before* a claim would have been generated by the ILS.

Desiderata and Enhancements for INNOPAC Reporting Features: A Checklist: Innovative Interfaces, Inc. is only one of many ILS vendors with online report writing capabilities. Its Create List (resulting in Review files based on one or more specific modules' record-types), Create Statistical Reports (counts of specified record fields), Fund Reports (hierarchical constructs of layers of fund records and fund report groups), and SCATT (circulation module volume counts by classification ranges) are all report features which have powerful results and are also rather complex to use. Although power and complexity in systems design tend to be directly proportional, it is sometimes possible to increase "user friendliness" (to use a much overworked phrase) while maintaining the efficacy of such complex reporting features. Here are some enhancement suggestions:

1. Have the search strategy permanently displayable with its run Create (d) List, rather than elsewhere with no necessary automatically labeled linkage.
2. Have the current Sort strategy *also* permanently displayable with the Create (d) List it sorts, just like the List (display) parameters currently are.
3. Have Created Statistical Reports savable; with any Booleanated Create (d) List counted also automatically posted, too.
4. Have Create (d) Statistical Report search strategies savable, just like the search strategies for Create (d) Lists are.
5. Have Create (d) Statistical Report strategies also permanently linked in display with the Statistical Report it created.
6. Have INNOPAC's Create (d) Lists Booleanation commands use standard mathematical-logical nested parentheses convention for forming and combining subsets, replacing INNOPAC (Release 11's), etc. implicit "OR-operator subset to the right end" conventions. Currently failure to observe the implicit left priority command nesting can readily result in inadvertently generating Or-ed sets when AND-ed ones are actually the searcher's goal. See Figure 2: "Search strategy statement #1 and #2, suggested nested-parentheses enhancement of current INNOPAC conventions" for examples of how more standardized nested parenthesize conventions could more cogently bracket OR-ed search statement subsets in ILSs such as INNOPAC. Without the nested parentheses delineating the second, three Or-ed subset, "search strategy statement #2" reads differently than search strategy statement #1 with the final subset, < AND STATUS ~ paid > now part of a Booleanated OR set.
7. Have any separate library organization, site, or "agency" (if any) and searchers signed-on initials/name as part of Created List and Created Statistical Report *names* and *strategies*.
8. Having a free text notes field-box associated with each of these sometimes-cryptic search strategies, sort, and list parameters would make defining the purposes and peculiarities of management information report writer creations easier for the occasional user.
9. Documenting more of the classic pitfalls of record listing and statistical report counting production, including, for example, the disparity which can arise between fund record assignment

statistical totals within *Order* record-based reports and *Fund* record-based Fund Report balances whenever fund record adjustments are made for credits and reconciliation "journalizing."

10. More precoordinated reporting capabilities. (Under INNOPAC User Group ballot consideration fall '97.) Narrow "canned supplies" of "hard wired" reports, i.e., ARL statistics, ALA Directory statistics.

11. More postcoordinated reporting capabilities: (Under INNOPAC User Group ballot consideration fall '97.) This is along the lines of a "wide open skies," *ad hoc*, free form-type flexible report writer feature approach.

·12. Have the following enhancements done with INNOPAC's SCATT Tables of class/call number ranges of circulation data, and the concomitant INNOPAC class/call number range counts of volume counts:

   a. Have full "Descriptions," with their associated call number ranges, available for autoloading or already present in default mode online in INNOPAC upon delivery.

   b. Provide ongoing full National Title Count compatibility and support available as at least a Product. This might not technically be an enhancement in the narrow sense, since in INNOPAC parlance a Product is a feature or service for which a site must pay extra.

   c. Make these class/call number range designation reports *far more prominently accessible* in Management Information submenus, either in Circulation Statistics submenu or even in a prominent collection analysis second-tier submenu right under Management Information, right along with "Create Statistical Reports," "Create Lists," and "Vendor Information" as they are now.

13. Rather than allowing ad hoc fund reports based on percentage of 100% plus spending, INNOPAC #11 limits ad hoc fund report comparisons reports to just 99% of appropriation expended. Fund records that are overspent by a certain percentage can't be retrieved by that percentage (see Figure 3).

Note that until/unless most of the above suggestions are realized, it will be necessary to carry out solely postcoordinated PC applications

FIGURE 2

"Search strategy statement #1 and #2, Suggested nested-parentheses enhancement of current INNOPAC conventions' examples"

(Note how a more standardized set of nested parenthesize conventions could more cogently bracket OR-ed search statement subsets in ILSs such as INNOPAC):

–Search strategy statement #1 (Suggested nested-parentheses enhancement for INNOPAC Management Reports module):
<(Fund code & Fund code) AND (ORDER TYPE OR ORDER TYPE OR ORDER TYPE") AND STATUS ~ paid.>

–Search strategy statement #2 (Current INNOPAC Release 11 convention):
INNOPAC #11 uses implicit left to right subset Booleanation this way: <Fund code = 11000 & Fund code 19999 AND ORDER TYPE = s OR ORDER TYPE = i OR ORDER TYPE = e AND STATUS ~ paid.>

FIGURE 3

"Rather than allowing ad hoc fund reports based on percentage of 100% plus spending, INNOPAC limits ad hoc reports to just 99%":

<You may locate all funds in Pullman Coll. Dev. Divs that have spent over or under a certain percentage of their appropriation.
Enter the percentage (1-99) _____
You may key up to nine fund codes for comparison.
Type <RETURN> at Fund code____? when done keying.
Fund code? _____>

based operations in order to preserve parameters and create ad hoc Reports. Options existing within the INNOPAC domain include doing print-out jobs of Create (d) Statistical Reports and other non-saved Create (d) List parameters, copy/paste them to other PC file outside of INNOPAC's domain, create them as attachments for email forwarding, create them as share files in a networked environment from one's PC, or park them in a subdirectory on the library's PC server.

The relationship between these two last precoordinated and postcoordinated enhancement proposal features is a complimentary one. Ideally, training parameters set up time should be afforded to library workers with enough prior time to fit together a local library approach to utilizing local institutional workflow adaptation, fixed code table development (especially with a trans-module perspective), and reportwriting, Create List, Create Statistical Reports, Fund Report hierarchy construction should all ideally be part of a one-year test procedure process prior to a two FY phase-in of a new system. Given that this will virtually never happen, however, the next best thing for report/statistical operations would be arranging for the full spectrum of management report, module operations to be much more expressly spelled out by system vendors through adequate documentation, tutorial features, and adequate online posting of all search strategy and display parameters, as noted above. If a librarian doing report writing just one or two or three times a year can't view the Booleanation strategy which generated an old Create List, or the Create List "sort" parameters, or the Create Statistical Reports sort and compile strategies online with the product of that strategy, then report/statistics writing and compilation might tend to gravitate toward a small team of elite management information experts.

In small libraries the constantly increasing complexity of management information and other modules may make some such complex ILS's unwieldy automatons, with vast yet untapped capacities for management information processing control and library service–unless online report writing functions much more fully, and helpfully spell out strategies in standard ways.

Browsing the INNOPAC Users Group's Web site's enhancement section reveals an (understandable) emphasis on smaller, detail-oriented enhancements, rather than on broader redesign proposals. However, a broader design philosophical orientation is also essential.

The "Payoff": The "Devil in the Details" Revealed

Having examined precoordination-postcoordination, hybridization, and some aspects of the organizational front of management report functions, let's now turn to review of various aspects of fund accounting and online report features.

Library fund accounting subsystems, especially in larger public and academic libraries, tend to be heavily laden, perhaps even burdened, by a plethora of detailed internal fund records, codes, and fund group reports. ILSs tend to also have code breakouts such as "order type" categories, which can serve as subfund breakout categories. These internal detailed fund structures and order type code breakouts are deserving of closer scrutiny, especially since their care and maintenance often takes much valuable time, and their intricacies are often a burden to the comprehension of the occasional user.

Detailed Cost Centered Fund Reporting: An Asset or a Debit?: It's a debit, basically. We spend a lot of time "shadow-fund-boxing." Biology monographs. Parent accounting agency budget codes strings and affixes. American History serials. French literature continuation series. Budget directors of libraries' parent accounting organizations are often amazed (and occasionally even impressed!) with our Library-world obsession with creating, maintaining, and reporting much more fund account data than just for the few parent accounting agency global budget lines, such as a university's "Science Subscriptions" budget or a public library's "Continuations" budget. The *de facto* replacement of detailed fund accounting by existing or nearly complete LCCN class-based breakouts of approval books at some University Libraries are no longer detail fund-accounted.

On the other hand, having said this about the clutter aspect of detailed cost center fund accounting however, I should point out that the temptation to use such features extensively can be high, especially when complex consortial or shared positive (allocated-out) or negative (allocated-to) split payments for large online services are being fund accounted year after year. In such circumstances the historical value of such fund accounting can be very useful. I have been considering using, for example, creating specific fund records solely to record credits that accrue as institutional funds external to a library's own set of funds. Such expenditure transfers in and out could then provide a detailed historical record to compare regular appropriations plus or minus expenditure transfer contributions to or from General, Director's reserve type detailed find record cost centers, solely to track the ins and outs of all kinds of accounts, like Fines money revolving funds, endowments. For example, proportionate Humanities vs. Social Science vs. branch campuses expenditure transfers to cover percentages of such multi-disciplinary databases as ProQuest, etc., on a general, reserve type budget.

Order Type-based "Subaccount" Reporting Possibilities: By order type subfunds I mean the arrangements wherein mono firm, mono replacement, mono form-approval, and mono book-approval order records for library materials are often broken out by material-type-like subaccounts. Biology or civil engineering, for example, might each have a number of breakouts of encumbrance and expenditure, by a variety of order types.

Not all systems provide equal report outcomes for their order typology. Some, like WLN ACQ, provide no adequate management reporting form the many order types and related data fields utilized on individual order records. The GEAC ACQ 8000 system provided only balances broken out within the funds designated as formal fund records. Generally, it is better to receive the benefits of balance totals, order record totals, and title-on-order lists without establishing, say, four formal fund accounts in biology monographs just to track firm, replacements, form-approvals, and book-approvals. This species of order subtypologies from fund account data does not necessarily translate well from one library acquisitions module to another, however. Parent organization accounting systems have no need for this breakout of data, or even for the single departmental cost center level account, let alone a plethora of suborder-type balances. Nor do vendors customarily provide a full cross-system compatible set of information in this area, unless order typology is embedded in fund accounting data. It does seem as though having parent accounting budgets, detailed shadow fund cost centers, *and a whole set of Order types as well* seems like excessive fund report clutter in a system. Fund accounting report managers might eventually be tempted to junk full-blown departmental type cost center fund code records (linked also to order types) in favor of just having a second tier of fused order type-detailed fund record like designations.

Transitions from one ILS acquisitions system or one material vendor's automated arrangement to another can result in changed fund accounting configurations.

Although postcoordinated-downloads from a networked system to desktop-based applications can provide in some configurations some of this data, the need for order type data, like much other fund account reporting, remains very library-specific.

"Foreign" and "Direct" designations are of comparable, if not greater interest for library management reporting. The ready grouping of orders by these categories are most often associated with vendor generated reports or with microcomputer application packages. These designations are classic desiderata, and could be "captured" through existing kinds of library acquisitions systems; either by predesigns of dedicated fields or by the elective use of freely definable note fields. In the Washington State University Libraries' "Ordering and Receiving" INNOPAC module usage of fixed code fillers, one of the open CODE fields is used at WSU to designate either a "U.S." or "Canadian-British-Continental" or "Other-Foreign" imprint of Order records. Easy identification of direct vs. vendor acquired orders, and domestic vs. (pricey) foreign imprints as classes of order records can be much need, but often unavailable. Special identifiers in each order record could change that! While the markers might not be classic "order types," such other identifier fields in order records have similar uses/features.

Fund accounting, accounts/payable and related financial reports are of course classic examples of online management reports, which readily spring to mind whenever "reports" are mentioned. Here I want to confine myself to a few miscellaneous, but major, points:

Difficulty in orienting level and location in fund report hierarchical "sandwiches": Fund report hierarchies, such as those consisting of layers of fund records sandwiched in between fund report "bundles" can be confusing to the non-reportologist. What lines are the labels of actual fund records, and which are mere report bundles? Exactly where does the display fit into a fund hierarchy? Some systems, such as INNOPAC do indicate the level down in the fund report hierarchy. Perhaps however, more explicit labeling by all ILS vendors could aid the occasional user in avoiding at least some of the confusion as to where the user is in a fund hierarchical maze?

Invoice breakouts by major fund divisions: One of the more complex features of vendor-library relations involves the batching of invoicing data by such large groupings as ship-to and large collection development divisions, such as the classic divisions of humanities, social science, and science. If the account number field, the FAXON "FISL," or the EBSCO "HEGIS" contains in part the necessary large division designation, then redesignation or subdivision of ship-to invoice groupings can be easy. Finessing management reporting for library customers can be a major activity for acquisitions librarians and vendor representatives.

Parent organization payment systems as "the" acquisition systems for libraries?: Consider, for example, this "thought experiment": imagine that suddenly your library has no "traditional" online acquisition module. How viable is a "typical" purchasing office/controller's office for use as a full purchasing-of-bibliographic-materials system? Some such functions are tried and true–others would be rather novel, at least in early use by a non-library parent accounting agency. The fund accounting of expenditures for major, global, collection development divisions such as the traditional "humanities-monographs" or "science serials" is already carried out, of course, by parent account/payment systems. (And order placements and payments functions are, of course, standard as well.) Name-address directories are commonly available in parent online systems, too.

Parent account/payment systems do not commonly fund account

the thousand-plus departmental cost centers utilized by many large libraries. Nor are encumbrances routinely recorded throughout the fiscal year on many parent account/payment systems, although carried-over-encumbrances (for grand book totals, etc.) are sometimes recorded at the end of a fiscal year as a practice in some institutions. To support many thousands of bibliographic records would be a large load for typical parent account/payment systems–such as the Washington State University "PAPR" system, for example (Jarvis, 1992). The idea of bypassing the middleman, interface needs of library acquisition department system modules and parent account systems by enhancing the parent account system's bibliographic and detailed fund accounting features is, in theory, one way to move toward the elimination, or "dis-integration" of the library acquisitions "module" as an integrated segment of an ILS (Ray, 1993).

CONCLUSION

Thomas Kuhn's schema of "normal sciences" and "paradigm shifts" outlined in his classic *The Structure of Scientific Revolutions* can readily be applied to the practice of "normal" library science as well (Kuhn, 1970). Our library information science paradigms are shifting rapidly, and in many directions. At the extreme end of possibilities perhaps no new set of paradigms will establish themselves as "normal science" for any significant period of time. Or perhaps the "compression" of the traditional library acquisitions module–PC report writer configuration as a result of materials vendor–libraries' parent financial agency will define a new paradigm of "normal" library science, at least for a period of time before yet another "normal library science" paradigm shift overthrows the prior standard paradigm. Consider the amount of time, money, and effort applied to the three-party cycle of library ILS acquisitions module *to* material vendor system *back-to* library acquisitions module *then-to* library's parent accounts payable agency then *back-to* the material vendor's accounts payable department. If there were no separate acquisitions module, then this four-phase process would be a two-phase one, barring claiming/non-fulfillment complications.

The technical systems dimensions of acquiring and coordinating the online management report will obviously continue to undergo extensive change as the thin client server environment of applets, servlets, and Web-source data continue to proliferate.

The "Hybridology" and "Organizational Front" aspects of acquiring adequate online management reportology are also challenges to our library professional work. Coordinating reportology has been demonstrated above as requiring extensive "quality time" from our profession, far more than it has been receiving. This whole library science subdiscipline of reportology covers a vast area, actually a complex set of major topics, that could readily fill volumes, and a series of ALA Preconferences as well!

Finally, we should acknowledge the universal requirement that all online systems and applications be more fully capable of instant canned report production, great flexibility for *ad hoc* report writing, and mixes/blends of these across the whole spectrum between a "pure" precoordination and postcoordination.

REFERENCES

American Library Association ALCTS CMDS Quantitative Measures for Collection Analysis Committee's North American Title Count Subcommittee discussion at 1997 ALA Midwinter meeting, Washington, DC; *also at*: ALA ALCTS Quantitative Measures for Quantitative Analysis Committee's Subcommittee on the North American Title Count Program, ALA 1998 Annual Meeting, Washington, DC.

Boss, Richard W. *Automating Library Acquisitions: Issues and Outlook*. Knowledge Industry Publications, White Plains, NY, 1982.

Boss, Richard W. "Technical Services Functionality in Integrated Library Systems," *Library Technology Reports*, Vol. 28, January/February 1992.

Corbin, John Boyd. *Managing the Library Automation Project*. The Oryx Press. Phoenix; 1985, pp. 84-85.

Jarvis, William E. Professional practice and observations of the author, 1988, Lehigh University Libraries, GEAC 8000 Acquisitions module fund accounting display structural trouble-shooting.

Jarvis, William E. Professional practice and observations of the author with GEAC 8000 Circulation module downloading of Lehigh's GEAC-based LC range-based total volume count to his PC-based Lotus spreadsheet, Lehigh University Libraries, 1988-89.

Jarvis, William E. "Managing preorder inventory files online: In pursuit of integrated workflows," *The Acquisitions Librarian*, Number 5, 1991, pp. 115-128. Published monographically in Katz, Bill, ed., *Vendors and Library Acquisitions*, (Binghamton, NY: The Haworth Press, Inc.) 1991, pp. 115-128.

Jarvis, William E. "Interactions between acquisitions system expenditure reports and university financial services payment systems: WLN ACQ to WSU's PAPR," *Library Acquisitions: Practice & Theory*, Vol. 16, 1992, pp. 405-410.

Kuhn, Thomas. *The Structure of Scientific Revolutions*. University of Chicago Press, Chicago, 1970, 2nd ed.

Ray, Ron. "The dis-integrating library system: Effects of new technologies in acquisitions," *Library Acquisitions: Practice & Theory*, Vol.17, Number 2, 1993, pp. 127-136.

APPENDIX A

"Management Information Services Librarian"

(A sample position description for coordinating in the contemporary, highly interconnected library systems environment.):

Coordinates and facilitates a wide variety of collection management activities, including the ILS's "management information" report features, statistical functions utilization, collection fund reporting, and serves as resource-person in overall collection analysis. Assists with assessments/statistics as requested, assists in monitoring fund accounts/budget expenditures, and assists in statistically-based vendor evaluation. Provides miscellaneous collection services support. Serves on Collection Development Committee and collegially communicates collection development and collection management concerns among the Libraries' groups and individuals.

APPENDIX B

"Example of Packaging a One Customer Create List Review File Using INNOPAC Features–A Briefing Note for the Veterinary/Pharmacy Library at WSU, Pullman"

(If this report to a client about a report appears somewhat confusing, bear in mind the amount of interpretation, editing, and "clean-up" often necessary in order to brief the occasional user/consumer of this kind of data. In other words, the confusion sometimes goes with the territory!):

****

From: Will Jarvis <jarvis@wsu.edu>
Subject: *Updated today* INNOPAC Review file, <wsujarvisVETSERpd7/ 96on6-12-98>, has 565 records posted in Griffin\Management Information\Create Lists\ #31. Also see below a Created Statistical Report based on that Booleanated Review file.

1. *Search* Strategy used: FUND between PAID DATE between 07-01-96 & 06-30-98 AND FUND between 16001 & 16999.

2. *Sort* Strategy used: Subscription or Continuation Order Type; then alpha by title: <List data from review file: wsujarvisVETSERpd7/96on6-12-98 >

LIST FORMAT

1 > Starting record? (1-565)	1
2 > Ending record? (1-565)	565
3 > Print field labels for variable length fields? (y/n)	n
4 > Start displaying each variable length field on a new line? (y/n)	y
5 > Number of blank lines between records. (1-4)	1
6 > Display meaning of fixed field, instead of value? (y/n)	n
7 > Page heading	–
8 > Print TITLE all in upper case? (y/n)	y
9 > Number items in list? (y/n)	n

****

3. *List* fields strategy used: ORD#, Title, ISSN, Order Type, Paid field amounts/date, compared fy 96/97/97/98 (to 6/12/98am only).

4. *To view* your review file: Go into <INNOPAC\Management Information\ Create Lists \Review File #31>, which is named <wsujarvisSERpd7/96on6-12-98>, a list of 565 Vet serial titles.

5. *Downloading/file transfer*: I do not usually recommend trying FTS emailing *larger* Review files from within Create Lists, but it can be done. I have just FTS-ed this 565 Order records Vet Review file to your davisb@wsu.edu email domain. If you would wish to try Copying from within Griffin Create List function, go ahead. Then try Pasting into WORD or some other MS application. You needn't in your case, since you have it in Microsoft-compatable Eudora application.

6. Discussion: This Review file from Create List function covers all of FY 96/97 and most of FY 97/98, i.e., payments through 2nd week of June 12, 1998. Thus it is a good history of Vet's 565 subscription & continuation mono series serial Order records that were paid since 7/1/96, w/a comparison of fy 96/97 "Paid" prices w/97/98 prices, *minus* anything expended from 6/12/98pm thru late June Fiscal Close of fy 97/98. (Most of what VET paid for in fy96/97 is of course also paid for in fy97/98, but not always.)

7. Created Statistical Report based on this Vet Review file #31 is Pasted right below here:

STATISTICS REPORT–wsujarvisVETSERpd7/96on6-12-98

Number of records processed: 565

Fund Name	# of Orders
16010	3
16800	450
16860	106

16861	1
16890	5

7. Statistical Report notes are:

    a. Based on a Booleanated Review file #31 (see above designations).

    b. Number of "Orders" was selected as the counted factor.

Will Jarvis, Librarian 3

Head, Acquisitions

Washington State Univ. Libraries

Pullman, WA 99164-5610

vox:509.335.2520

fax:509.335.9589

<jarvis@wsu.edu>

APPENDIX C

"Example of a Desiderata List of Management Reports"

(A list of needs identified at Washington State University Libraries in 1993 for possible use in a proposed developmental online project. The project was not realized. Please consider this as just a rough draft guide checklist.):

LIST OF MANAGEMENT REPORTS

The following is the list of management reports for the System:[1]
Acquisitions:[2]

    1. Monographic Vendor Receipt Performance Report (Expected date vs Arrival date)

    2. Title Preorder Report

    3. Title Order Report

    4. Title Receipt Report

    5. Serials Vendor Receipt Performance Report (Expected date vs Received date)

    6. Fund Account Balance Report

    7. Title Inventory Report (General inventory may contain all Acquisitions data)

    8. Cancellation Report

    9. New Title Report

    10. Detailed Encumbrance & Expenditures Report

    11. Encumbrance & Expenditure Summary Report

    12. Vendor Claim Fulfillment Performance Report (refers to items claimed only)

13. Title Report by Order Type

14. Serials Title Inventory by Account Number Report (includes amount of last payment)

15. System Activity Report[3]
    a. Number of titles set up by material type
    b. Number of titles in process
    c. Number of items received by material type
    d. Number of items claimed by material type
    e. Number of items withdrawn
    f. Number of items canceled by material type
    g. Number of items auto-reordered

16. Multiple Requested Title Report

17. Annual Serial Price Change Report

18. Historical Average & Total Price Change Report

19. Expenditures by location by call number class by cost center

Binding:

1. Bound Title Report
2. Binding Expenditures Report (by location by cost center)
3. Rebound Title Report
4. Binding Activity Report by location[4]
    a. Number of items bound
    b. Number of items rebound
    c. Number of items returned

---

[1] Please note that any activity reporting will be collected and summarized for requested time periods.

[2] Presently not an active system

[3] Presently only available for Serials Control

[4] Presently available in Serials Control

Circulation:

1. Circulation Activity Report by location[5]
    a. Number of items circulated by call number class
    b. Number of items circulated by patron type
    c. Number of items circulated by call number class by material type
    d. Number of items circulated by use type
    e. Number of user requested holds by user type
    f. Number of internal charges
    g. Total fines by location by call number class by patron type
    h. Number of holds canceled

2. High Activity Title Report
3. Inactive Title Report
4. Circulation Exception Report by location[6]
    a. Unlinked item report
    b. Report of items circulated requiring an override
    c. Manual fines or credits
    d. Report of items held requiring an override
    e. Report of items automatically discharged
    f. SNAG Report
5. Interlibrary Loan Activity Report
    a. Monographs
    b. Periodicals (esp. copyrighted items)
6. Reserve Title Report
7. Held Item Report
8. Patron Inventory Report
9. Patron Fine History
10. Mass Renewal Report

Database Maintenance:

1. Title Replacement Report
2. External Source Load Title Report
3. System Activity Report by location
    a. Number of titles process by process type (added, replaced, deleted, up-graded)
    b. Number of titles processed by process type by individual
    c. Number of titles loaded (from tape, imported, etc.) by origin
    d. Number of titles replaced
    e. Number of titles deleted
    f. Number of titles process by material type
    g. Number of titles withdrawn
    h. Number of titles processed locally (added or modified)
    i. Number of new barcodes added
    j. Number of new call numbers added
    k. Number of authority changes (added, replaced, deleted, upgraded)
4. Withdrawn Title Report by location
5. Title list of non-upgraded materials
6. Title Inventory of Missing Items by location
7. GPO Biennial Survey

---

[5] Available, totals will be included as part of all collected statistics
[6] Available

General:

1. On-line Catalog Activity Report
   a. Number of catalog searches by search category
   b. Number of catalog searches by location
   c. Remote Sessions Report
      i. Average time per session
      ii. Total time for all sessions
      iii. Total number of sessions
      iv. Number of searches by search category
   e. Number of catalog search hits by call number
   f. Report of catalog searches with no hits/max. hits
   g. External database accesses by database
   h. Session scripts or logs containing search, search type, results, time stamp, location, etc.
2. Library System Use Report
   a. Report of computer transactions
   b. Report of computer resources expended
   c. Hourly system activity and response time
   d. Transaction logs or scripts (contains search, search type, results, etc.)
   e. System error report
   f. User comment report
3. Shelf List Title Report
4. ARL Report
5. Title Inventory by location (primary, secondary, tertiary)
6. National Shelf List Count
7. Manuscripts National Catalog Report
8. Employee Expenditure Reports
9. American Library Directory Report

Serials Control:

1. Vendor Claim Report by title
2. System Activity Report by location
   a. Number of items received
   b. Number of items claimed
   c. Number of items not received
   d. Active titles

3. Vendor Claim Report by title
4. Active Serials Report

Tools:

1. General report writer for ADHOC reports
   a. Uses standard set of data element for selection
   b. Allows user selection of sort elements
   c. Allows user selection of report titles
   d. Allows user selection of report total
2. Ability to select information for downloading
3. Collection of historical data from all areas for ADHOC reports

Source: WSUL Management Reports Task Force's LIST OF MANAGEMENT REPORTS, 1993, Pullman, WA

Index

Abstracts
  on art, 35,40
  for serials, 9,10f,27
Academic books
  fund accounting for, 78-80
  purchasing considerations for,
    78-80, 86-87
  titles reports of, 78-79,85-87
  vendors of, 78-79
ACCESS database, for management
    data integration, 69
Access management
  concerns about, 23-24,26
  as hybrid process, 132-133
Accuracy, concerns about, 23-25
Acquisitions librarianship. *See also*
    Collection management
  accounting information for. *See*
    Fund accounting
  decision support systems for, 47-53
  Integrated Library Systems for,
    76-77, 107,130-131,146
  management information needs of,
    5-7,41,44
    hybrid report formats for,
      126-148
  medical journals example, 65-73
  scope of, 1-2,107
  in secondary education setting, 30,
    37-38,44-45
  vendor's relationship with, 104-107
Ad hoc report writing, 126,136,147
Advertisements, in online databases,
    25
AGRI-COLA, faculty assessment of,
    36-37
ALCTS. *See* Association for Library
    Collections and Technical
    Services

Allied health, Brandon/Hill titles
    report of, 15
Allocation, in fund accounting, 80-82,
    85,143
Alphabetical titles list, for serials, 12
American Library Association (ALA)
  public library data from,
    41,131-132
  serials titles and, 11,12f
American Standard Code for
    Information Interchange
    (ASCII), 26,32
AMIGOS Collection Analysis, 52
ANSI standards, for library statistics,
    46
Applied Science and Technology
    Index, faculty assessment of,
    35,40
Approval plans, for book selection
  categories of, 106
  evaluation of, 57-60
  system management reports for,
    60-64
Archive lists, storage options for, 137
Art Abstracts, faculty assessment of,
    35,40
ArticleFirst, faculty assessment of, 35,
    40
Articles, online databases of, 24-25
Articles Accessed Report, 19
Articles Purchased Report, 19
ASCII. *See* American Standard Code
    for Information Interchange
Association for Library Collections
    and Technical Services
    (ALCTS), serials titles and,
    11,12f
Authority lists, for serial titles, 6
Automation

definition of, 3
design importance of, 66-68,70-73,
    116,118
faculty assessment of, 29-40
uniform reporting requirements for,
    131-132
Order activity, for serials, 7,26
Order records
    as accounting subfunds, 143-144
    INNOPAC cross-referencing of,
        137-138,140
Organizational culture
    decision support systems and,
        49-50
    hybrid reporting and, 134-136
Out-of-print books, 95-99,101,
    105-106
Ownership management, as hybrid
    process, 132-133
Oxford English Dictionary, faculty
    assessment of, 35,40

Paper. *See* Printed material
Parent account/payment systems,
    145-146
Percentage Based Allocations (PBA),
    for library materials budget,
    52-53
Periodicals. *See* Journals; Serials
Personal computers (PC)
    hybrid report formats and, 140-141
    spreadsheet download formats for,
        125,130,132
Personnel requirements
    for hybrid management
        information,
        126-128,134-136
    for serials control, 109-111,111f
Philosophical perspectives, 125-148
Poetry journals, online databases of,
    25
PORTALS (Portland Area Library
    System)
    administrative perspectives of, 91

cooperative projects of, 91-93
members of, 90-91
purpose of, 90
Postcoordination, in hybrid reports,
    127-131,140-141
Pre-order searching, for academic
    books, 76,78
Precoordination, in hybrid reports,
    127-131,140-141
Price information
    on academic books, 78-79,86
    hybrid formats for, 129-130
    on medical journals, 65-73
    on serials, 6,8,9,16
    vendor's tracking of, 104-105,107
Printed material
    continued interest in, 34,36-37
    database systems versus,
        22,24-25,45
    faculty transitions away from,
        30,34, 36-37
Printing process
    for academic books, 77-79
    for journals, delays in, 116
Privacy protection, concerns about, 19
ProQuest Direct®, as periodical
    database, 21-28
PsychLit, faculty assessment of, 35,40
Publication Report, for serials
    acquisitions, 19
Publisher Report, for serials
    acquisitions, 19
Publisher titles reports
    for academic books, 78-79,85,87
    for serials, 11
Publishers
    academic book purchasing from,
        78-79,85,87
    book selection plans and, 58,63
    of serials, information needs of, 5-7
    vendor's relationship with, 104-106
Purchase method, for book selection
    plans, 61
Purchase vouchers, for fund
    accounting, 85-86
Purchasers, statistical reports on, 7,26

Readability, concerns about, 24
Reportology
  in collection management
      coordination, 134-136
  definition of, 2,4,127
  hybridization of, 132-133
  INNOPAC enhancements for,
      137-142
  postcoordination in, 127-131,
      140-141
  precoordination in,
      127-132,140-141
Research strategies, with electronic
      resources, 33-34,36-37,40
Returned books
  accounting for, 79-80
  vendor tracking of, 106
Richard Abel Company, 104

Sales reports, for vendors, 105-106
SCATT, as INNOPAC enhancement,
      138-142
Scholarly journals, online databases
      of, 24,26
SCOPE (Subject Classification of
      Periodicals) serial titles
      reports, 8,17f,18
Search strategies
  in INNOPAC, 119,134-135,
      137,139,141f
  in online databases, 33-34
SearchBank Usage Statistics, of
      Information Access
      Company, 29,32,36,40
Serialist listserv, 113
Serials. *See also* Journals
  automated control modules for,
      109-110,114
  claims for missing,
      110-116,111f-113f
  online reports for, 5-20,22-27
  weeding arrangement, of
      PORTALS, 91-92
Serials claiming
  automation of, 109-112,111f-112f,
      114,116
  fill rate of, 113,115

prematurity in, 112-113,113f
  statistical reports on, 110-114,
      111f-113f
  success factors for, 115-116
  survey on, 113-116
Serials management information
  Data Research Associates reports
      for, 44
  Dawson Group reports for, 17-19
  Faxon Company reports for,
      7-17,10f, 12f,14f-15f,17f
  future development partnerships
      for, 19-20
  for medical journals, 65-73
  needs for, 5-7,42-43
  vendor databases for, 6-7,12-13,69
Short articles, online databases of, 25
SilverPlatter's management reports,
      faculty assessment of, 29,
      31-32
Social Sciences Index, faculty
      assessment of, 35,40
Spreadsheet formats, for management
      reports, 32,59,129,132
Standing orders, for book selection,
      58,62-63,105-106
State University of New York
      (SUNY), decision support
      systems in, 51
Statistical reports
  for book selection plans, 58-59
  for collection management, 92-93
      hybrid formats for, 134-142
  on document delivery, 7,26,38
  Florida College Center package of,
      43-45
  for library management, 6-7,41-46
      INNOPAC system for,
          117,119-123, 137-142
      Integrated Library System and,
          42, 44-45
  on online behavior, 7,17-19,26-27
  on serials claiming, 110-114,
      111f-113f
  system criteria for, 123
  for vendors, 7,26,105-106

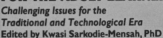

 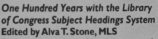